PERFORMANCE
EDITIONS

TCHAIKOVSKY

THE SEASONS
Opus 37bis

Edited and Recorded by Alexandre Dossin

To access companion recorded performances online, visit:
www.halleonard.com/mylibrary

Enter Code
2983-5144-2650-2464

On the cover:
Winter Landscape, or Russian Winter (1827)
by Nikifor Stepanovich Krylov
(1802–1831)

ISBN 978-1-4234-5809-8

www.halleonard.com

Contact Us:
Hal Leonard
7777 West Bluemound Road
Milwaukee, WI 53213
Email: info@halleonard.com

In Europe contact:
Hal Leonard Europe Limited
42 Wigmore Street
Marylebone, London, W1U 2RN
Email: info@halleonardeurope.com

In Australia contact:
Hal Leonard Australia Pty. Ltd.
4 Lentara Court
Cheltenham, Victoria, 3192 Australia
Email: info@halleonard.com.au

CONTENTS

The price of this publication includes access to companion recorded performances online, for download or streaming, using the unique code found on the title page. Visit **www.halleonard.com/mylibrary** and enter the access code.

HISTORICAL NOTES

Pyotr Il'yich Tchaikovsky (1840–1893)

One of Russia's most beloved composers, Pyotr Il'yich Tchaikovsky was born in Votkinksky in 1840. A very sensitive child, he was attracted to poetry and music at a very early age; however, his musical education during his formative years was not very disciplined. After moving to St. Petersburg in 1850, Tchaikovsky was a student at the School of Jurisprudence from 1852–1859 and started working at the Ministry of Justice in 1860. Job security notwithstanding, his passion for music proved to be stronger, and he decided to make it his career. In 1859 the Russian Musical Society was created, and soon after (1862) the St. Petersburg Conservatory offered its first classes. Tchaikovsky enrolled at the conservatory and after his graduation in 1865 was invited by Nikolay Rubinstein (brother of Anton Rubinstein, the founder of St. Petersburg Conservatory) to be a professor in the newly created Moscow Conservatory in 1866, where he taught until 1878. Financially supported by Nadezhda von Meck from 1877 until 1890, Tchaikovsky quit his conservatory position and was able to concentrate exclusively on his work as a composer. He died in 1893 of cholera.

Tchaikovsky is the composer of masterpieces such as the *Nutcracker* and *Swan Lake* ballets, the Piano Concerto in B-flat minor, the Symphony No. 6 in B minor ("Pathétique"), and many other widely recognized works. His passion for Russia is evident in all his works, many of which use folk themes; nevertheless, Tchaikovsky found a perfect balance between Russian and Western European styles, making his works accepted and admired both in Russia and internationally.

As a proof of Russia's admiration for his work, its most famed musical institution, the Moscow Conservatory, was renamed Tchaikovsky Conservatory in 1940, in honor of the composer's 100th birthday. Within its walls, the first Tchaikovsky International Competition was held in 1958. This competition, whose first winner in the piano category was Van Cliburn, happens every four years and is considered as one of the most distinguished musical events in the world.

LABORUM DULCE LENIMEN G. SCHIRMER

PERFORMANCE NOTES

The topic of seasons and/or months of the year inspired many composers from different centuries. A short list would certainly include at least two great orchestral masterpieces: Vivaldi's *Four Seasons* (1723) for violin and orchestra, and Haydn's oratorio *The Seasons* (1799–1801). Piano works dedicated to this topic include *Le Mois, Op. 74* (1874, with a few pieces composed in 1838) by Charles-Valentin Alkan, *Das Jahr* (1841) by Fanny Hensel, and two works by Judith Zaimont: *Calendar Collection* (1976) and *A Calendar Set* (1972–1978). Tchaikovsky's set is the only one incorrectly named, since his cycle is not divided in four seasons, as one would expect; a more appropriate name would be "The Months," like in Alkan, or "The Year," like in Hensel and Zaimont.

Even though Tchaikovsky composed a great number of solo piano music, by far his most famous piano work is the First Piano Concerto. His two piano sonatas, very extensive and demanding works, never entered the standard piano repertoire. The majority of his piano works are small pieces, often included in groups, such as opp. 19, 21, and 51 (six pieces each), op. 40 (twelve pieces), op. 72 (eighteen pieces), and the collection *Album for the Young,* Op. 39 (with twenty-four pieces). Not all works were assigned an opus number and it is not clear why *The Seasons* was given op. 37bis, when it was composed before op. 37 (Sonata in G Major).

Among the numerous cycles of small pieces, certainly *The Seasons* occupy a very special place in Tchaikovsky's output. The twelve pieces were commissioned in 1875 by Nikolay Bernard, the publisher of the journal *Nouvellist*. Tchaikovsky accepted the commission and sent the works as scheduled. The subtitles were all suggested by Bernard, as were the poetic epigraphs. It is worth noticing that most epigraphs were added later (the only ones included in the autograph are "January" and "March"), so we should not think of them as programs.

Tchaikovsky's writing for piano is not very idiomatic, especially when compared with pianists-composers such as Rachmaninoff or Prokofiev. A prolific and expert orchestral composer, Tchaikovsky naturally gravitated toward orchestral texture when composing for piano. This characteristic may explain why there are several successful orchestrations of *The Seasons* composed by Alexander Gauk, David Matthews, Vaclav Trojan, and Peter Breiner (Breiner's version is for violin and orchestra). For this reason when performing such works, one should use a great deal of imagination in order to effectively "orchestrate" the pieces and convey an orchestral sound out of the instrument. I strongly encourage anyone interested in performing *The Seasons* to listen to the great orchestral works by Tchaikovsky, as well as the different orchestrations of the cycle, paying close attention to the way the instruments are used.

These twelve works may be performed as a cycle (with a duration of around 45 minutes) or in small groups, a few pieces at a time. When performing them in small groups, I suggest playing at least four pieces, choosing one from each season. (My favorite group is "May," "August," "October," and "December.") Such groupings have timings around 15–17 minutes and work very well in a recital setting. In my opinion, performing only one piece at a time works well only as an encore—"October" works particularly well after the B-flat minor concerto!—but not in a recital program. These pieces are very simple and of a small scope, and they tend to feel even smaller when accompanied by other major works.

The Seasons is certainly among the most popular solo piano works by Tchaikovsky. In Russia, these works are often performed and are beloved by musicians and audiences alike. In spite of their technical simplicity, the performance of a group from *The Seasons* is required during the Tchaikovsky International Piano Competition and as part of the third-year piano examinations in the Tchaikovsky Conservatory, both in Moscow, Russia.

General Observations

Metronome markings

Metronome markings are editorial. Instead of suggesting a specific marking, I decided to provide a small range of possible tempos. Performances outside those markings may lack the necessary clarity (if too fast) or may not allow for correct phrasing (if too slow).

Fingering

Fingerings are editorial and have in mind a medium-sized hand. Some adjustments may need to be made for smaller hands. In some instances, the hand distribution has been changed in order to allow for smoother pedaling. These changes are all editorial, since Tchaikovsky did not include any performance indications of this kind in his autograph. As a rule, fingerings were chosen in order to convey the phrasing and articulation, not for comfort. Two numbers connected by a dash (for example, 1-1) represent a slide between black and white keys. Two numbers connected by a slur, as it is common practice, represent a finger substitution. In some cases, an optional fingering is shown in parenthesis.

Pedaling

All pedal markings are editorial. This edition follows the example of other editions regarding pedaling: it is only indicated where extremely important or for a specific effect. It is omitted altogether in sections where effective pedaling is almost impossible to notate or too obvious. One should assume that pedal needs to be used for most of the time. One way to approach this issue is: good pedaling is not supposed to be heard. In other words, use the pedal in such a way that the textures are always clear and not compromised by excessive blurring. The orchestral textures should be carefully practiced and the result should reflect the polyphonic richness of these works.

Dynamics and Articulation

Dynamics and articulation are original. In the few instances where there are editorial suggestions, they are in parenthesis.

Sources

This edition is based on the facsimile of Tchaikovsky's autograph, except for "April" (the autograph of which has been lost). Also consulted were the Muzyka edition (Moscow, 1989), Dover Publication *The Seasons and Other Works for Piano* (1996), which bases its version of *The Seasons* on a 1904 C.F. Peters edition, and another Russian edition—Moscow: Muzgiz, 1948 (reprinted in New York by Edwin F. Kalmus, c. 1970).

Notes on Performing the Individual Pieces

January: At the Fireside

The opening piece of this cycle could not be "cozier": Tchaikovsky sets the mood for a cold winter night in Russia and invites us to sit by the fireplace. The gentle, E-major initial section looks as if it had been written for a string quartet. By adding a rest under the first note, Tchaikovsky leaves no doubt about the polyphonic texture he is aiming at. This section (ending on m. 29) needs to be performed with a soft but intense touch; special attention should be given to the articulation, and the editorial fingering has that purpose in mind. A medium-slow attack of the key will provide the string-quartet quality.

The middle section changes the overall polyphonic texture for a more soloistic one; use your imagination and choose the best sound for the repeated descending scale on m. 30, and similar. The arpeggio found on m. 31 (and sim.) should be played with a light touch, using half pedal in order to convey a harp sound. Three layers are clear in the next section (mm. 38–46), requiring a very exact voicing between the melodic, eighth-note bass notes and the arpeggiated figure in-between. The "A" section is identical to the beginning; the only difference consists in the lack of a measure (analogue to m. 18 in the first "A" section). Even though m. 18 is included in the autograph, there are doubts regarding its correctness. This measure creates an extra, unnecessary repetition of the motive; in all the other pieces from this cycle, there are no such departures from the norm. Therefore, one could argue that it was a mistake and that the "extra measure" should not be played. Many editions and most performers simply omit it. (Among the several performances I am familiar with, only Vaclav Newman's orchestration repeats that measure.) By looking at the autograph, one notices that m. 18 is at the beginning of a new line, which may have caused the mistake of rewriting it.

In the same way, mm. 51–52 are added to this edition (following the Russian editions as well as performance practice in Russia) despite the fact that they were not in the autograph. In the autograph, Tchaikovsky crosses out two measures right after m. 47—it looks like he meant to write the ascending triplet figure and wrote the descending instead. One could speculate that those two measures were not included by mistake, since their absence creates a lack of proportion in the section, something very unlikely in Tchaikovsky's style. That's probably the reason why many recordings keep the tradition of performing those two measures.

February: Carnival

A very beloved Russian religious tradition, *Maslenitsa* (from the word *maslo*, meaning butter) happens in the period of the year immediately preceding Lent. Before getting ready to fast, Russians eat lots of *bliny* (pancakes). This fast, spirited piece is one of the most difficult in the cycle (together with "November" and, to some extent, "September"). Define the articulation in mm. 1–2 by carefully using your wrists (move down in the first chord in the slur, and up in the second—the same technique should be used when accents are added in mm. 9, 10, and sim.) and holding the quarter notes, as notated by the stems. The sixteenth notes in mm. 3 and 4 should be played with a crisp staccato touch. Short imitative figures abound in this piece, and should be brought out: mm. 27–28, 35–42, and to a lesser extent mm. 3 and 4. Again, thinking in terms of orchestration can help one achieve that goal.

The down–up wrist motion described above is also important in the middle section, where its speed becomes twice slower (two quarter notes instead of four eighth notes in one bar). In the same way, the imitation between right and left hands (or different instruments) continues, as exemplified in mm. 89–93. I recommend practicing the imitations by playing the motives at the same time; you will then be able to check whether they are being shaped in the same way. In mm. 117–120, define clearly the difference between the two voices in the left hand.

It is interesting to observe that the only time Tchaikovsky used *fff* in the whole cycle is at the end of "February." Use relaxed, heavy hands and pedal to enhance your dynamic range (without making the staccato notes too "wet").

March: Song of the Lark

This is a peaceful, descriptive miniature. Only forty-six measures long, this is the shortest piece in the cycle. The overall dynamic should not exceed *mp*. Note that the *poco più f* in m. 11 does not mean *forte*, but "a little louder." That would take us from *p* to around *mezzo-piano*. The same exercise suggested for the practice of imitative sections should be used here: play the right hand in mm. 3–4 together with the left hand in mm. 5–6, making sure that the shaping and articulation are exactly the same.

From m. 11 to m. 30, use a fast attack in your right hand, with the goal of imitating the birdlike quality of the melodic line. Grace notes should be crisp and fast, almost played simultaneously with the main note. This piece works better in four: 4/8 instead of 2/4.

April: Snowdrop Flower

Those of us who have lived through the harshness of a Russian winter know very well the special feeling that the arrival of the first spring flowers brings. The original Russian title *Podsnezhnik* means the first flowers to show up, still "under the snow" (the literal translation of *Podsnezhnik*). In my opinion, the main difficulty in this piece is the chordal accompaniment figure. The repeated chords (mostly in the left hand, but at times alternating with right hand as well) can easily become too repetitive and take over the main melodic material. I suggest the practice of the accompaniment pattern by itself, paying attention to the "rebound" feeling. One should not think of each chord as a down motion, but rather slightly energize the first and second beats, and play the remaining beats as rebound motions.

The typical instrumental imitations occur in this work as well (see mm. 37–38 and mm. 39–40). For suggestions on how to best convey those ideas, see comments for "February" and "March."

May: White Nights

Loosely translated as "Summer Nights," a more literal translation from the Russian would be "White Nights," a reference to the long days and short nights in the high latitudes of Moscow and St. Petersburg. During the months of June and July, particularly, St. Petersburg celebrates the "white nights," a time of year the sun barely sets before immediately rising again. With this kind of inspiration, Tchaikovsky describes the inner feeling of reawakening that is felt by Russians every spring, after the long and severe winters. The arpeggios in the main theme should be played gently, as if playing a guitar.

The key of B-flat major appears without preparation, after the fermata on m. 9. I suggest a slightly faster attack for that section (when compared to the beginning of the piece), in order to get a brighter sound, enhancing this beautiful harmonic change. The tie on m. 16, right hand, was added by the editor by comparison with m. 83. Performance practice in Russia uses this tie on m. 16, and a careful observation of the autograph facsimile shows a little blur between the notes. The tie is very clear in m. 83. In mm. 17–19 and similar measures at the end, close attention should be paid to the rests in the left hand. The right hand should sustain its note for the duration of the measure, while the left hand releases exactly as notated.

Measure 20 introduces a new section: *Allegretto giocoso*. As always, please pay close attention to the polyphonic texture clearly notated by Tchaikovsky. There are four clear layers until m. 27, when one is dropped. Play the sixteenth notes in mm. 21 and 23 side-by-side; you will then be able to hear them better when you perform the complete texture.

June: Barcarole

Together with "October" and "November," this is probably one of the more often performed works from this cycle. Somewhat following the examples set by Mendelssohn in his "Venetian Boat Songs," Tchaikovsky provides an accompaniment figure that is undulating and repetitive, in order to create the "watery" feeling of this lovely work. Once again, we have several moments of imitation among the hands (mm. 4 and 5 and sim.). The polyphonic texture is further developed in the dynamic reprise, when the left hand has a beautiful countermelody (mm. 54–55, 58–59, and sim.). Throughout this piece, it is very important to differentiate between the melodic notes and the accompanying chords, as notated by Tchaikovsky with stems pointing down (mm. 4–12). The soloist (right hand) has a very emotional moment starting at m. 12, marked *poco più forte.* Here, Tchaikovsky adds tenuto markings on the eighth-note ascending scales. Use arm weight and slightly detach each note in those scales. Dynamic markings should be clearly followed.

An "orchestral" crescendo is needed from m. 32 until m. 39, preparing the next brief section (called *Allegro giocoso* in some editions). Hold the quarter notes of the syncopated left hand (mm. 32–39) for the entire length—this will enhance the rhythmic drive of those measures. The same applies to the final measures (mm. 91 to the end).

July: Song of the Reaper

The overall chordal texture of this piece reflects the strong energy displayed by the reapers in the height of the Russian summer. Play this with a "foot-stomping," masculine quality, from the beginning until m. 32. From there until the end, play gradually softer, as if you were walking away from the reapers, with their song getting quieter with the distance. Tchaikovsky achieves this effect not only by the use of diminuendo, but also by changing the left hand to a smoother texture in eighth-note triplets. This piece works better in two, or in cut-time (2/2).

August: Scherzo (Harvest)

Called "Scherzo" in the autograph, this piece is a continuation of the topic explored in "July." The main difference is the moving, fleeting texture in the "A" section. The overall dynamic should be *piano*, with a few outbursts to *forte*. Articulation should be very precise, observing the short "down–up" motions in both hands (mm. 1–3 and sim.). This should be carefully contrasted with the accents and staccato chords (mm. 4–8 and sim.). The first section ends with very pianistic arpeggios and octaves. The middle section should be played as a duo between the descending right-hand (mm. 68–75) and the ascending left-hand lines. The duo appears in stretto starting at m. 84 until it is restated at m. 100. Avoid the temptation to play the middle section too slow; a little flexibility is possible, but Tchaikovsky's indication (*Dolce cantabile*) does not ask for a change in tempo. Throughout this section, pay attention to the articulation—in the transition passage to the reprise, the articulation is what creates the unity between the main sections.

September: The Hunt

Octaves, double thirds, leaps, repeated chords—such are the technical demands for this powerful miniature. Pianists with small hands will find it very challenging to perform this work. The best approach when practicing "September" is to have very supple wrists combined with firm fingers. Try to find the shape of each chord in the air, before you touch the keys, and use your fingers as "forks," actively changing your position as you move around the chords. Keep an orchestral, full tone from the beginning until the end of m. 32. Starting from that point, individual instrumental lines and imitation appear, with an overall *piano* dynamic. Be very precise with the articulation in this section, and build up the energy starting at m. 41, culminating in the *ff* B-major chords (mm. 57–58).

October: Autumn Song
Tchaikovsky is very clear about the general mood of this piece with the tempo marking: *Andante doloroso e molto cantabile*. October is usually a cold month in Russia, and the nostalgic feeling of long and warm days disappearing for an extended period of time makes this piece very sad. Once more, Tchaikovsky's polyphonic writing is noticeable: after the first eight measures, the main melody appears in the left hand, while the right hand has a very expressive countermelody. The melodic material probably inspired Bernard in his choice of the poetic epigraph, "yellow leaves fly on the wind." See, for example, mm. 22–25: the melodic contour describes an overall downward motion, but with gentle motions up, such as the motions of a falling leaf.

November: Troika
By the time November arrives, it is clear that the Russian winter has come to stay. Snow abounds, and the image of a "Troika" (a sled pulled by three horses, usually with bells hanging by their necks) is very Russian. One of the most popular pieces in the cycle (often performed by Rachmaninoff as an encore), this is arguably the most difficult. Less polyphonic in general, "Troika" is very descriptive; the bells appear for the first time in the middle section in m. 30. They come back in the dynamic reprise, when the main theme is played by the left hand, while the right hand has fast staccato sixteenth notes.

December: Christmas
The last piece in this cycle is a very simple and candid little waltz, dedicated to this special period of the year (called in Slavonic countries *Sviatky*). In order to convey the phrasing, it is very important to think of it in 6/4, not 3/4 (every two measures make up one "hyper-measure"). In an almost Schubertian way, Tchaikovsky ends the first section in A-flat major, and by changing A-flat enharmonically to G-sharp he writes the middle section in E major. Here, the historical notion of "Trio" is apparent: after the ostinato pattern of a waltz throughout the first section, the trio becomes more soloistic, with three, clear melodic lines.

At the end of the Coda, it is very important not to make any ritardando, allowing the work to end naturally. Following the editorial pedaling at that moment allows for a nice, uplifting end to this piece and for the cycle as a whole.

—Alexandre Dossin

References

Sources and Suggested Reading:

In English:
Abraham, Gerald. *Tchaïkovsky; A Short Biography*. London: Duckworth, 1945.

Garden, Edward. *Tchaikovsky*. London: J.M. Dents and Sons Ltd., 1973.

Warrack, John Hamilton. *Tchaikovsky*. New York: C. Scribner's Sons, 1973.

In Russian:
Kunin, Y.F. *P.I. Tchaikovsky o kompozitorskom masterstve*. Moskva: Gossudartsvennoye Muzikalnoye Izdatelstvo, 1952.

Polyakova, L. *Vremena Goda Tchaikovskogo*. Moskva: Gossudartsvennoye Muzikalnoye Izdatelstvo, 1960.

Scores:

Facsimile of the autograph:
Tchaikovsky, P. *Vremena Goda*. Moscow: Muzyka, 1978.

Other editions:
Tchaikovsky, P. *Vremena Goda*. Moscow: Muzgiz, 1948.

Tchaikovsky, P. *Vremena Goda*. Moscow: Muzyka, 1989.

Tchaikovsky, P. *The Seasons and Other Works for Piano*. Mineola, NY: Dover Publications, 1996.

Recording Credits

Lance Miller, Recording Engineer
Alexandre Dossin, Producer and Performer
Recorded at Beall Concert Hall, University of Oregon School of Music and Dance

THE SEASONS

Времена Года
Vremena Goda

January: At the Fireside
Январь: У камелька
Ianvar': U kamel'ka

И мирной неги уголок
Ночь сумраком одела,
В камине гаснет огонёк,
И свечка догорела.
А. Пушкин

A little corner of peaceful bliss,
the night dressed in twilight;
the little fire is dying in the fireplace,
and the candle has burned out.
Aleksandr Pushkin

Pyotr Il'yich Tchaikovsky
Op. 37bis, No. 1

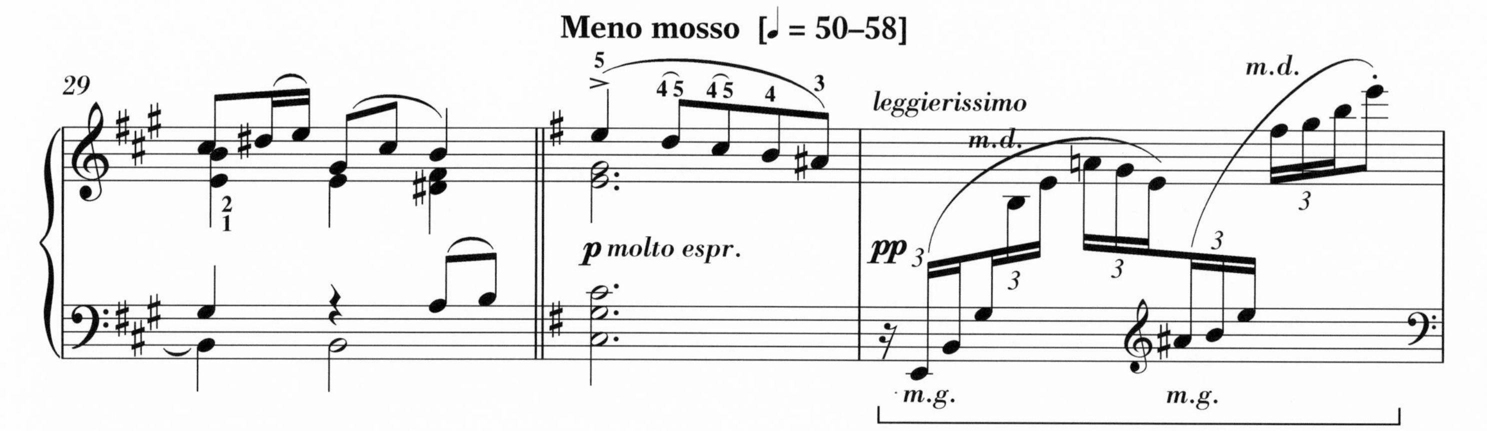

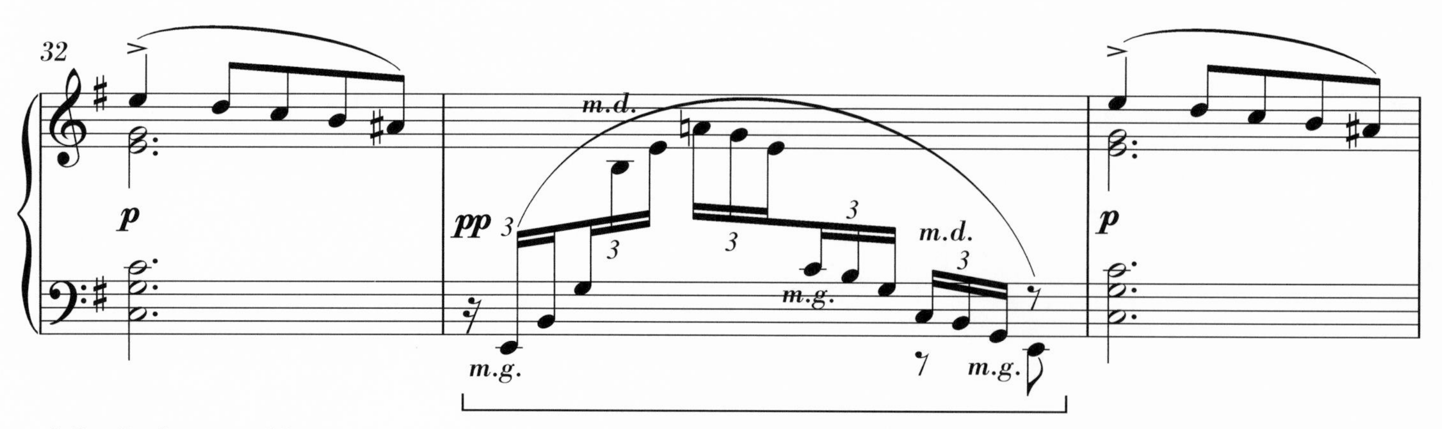

* See Performance Notes

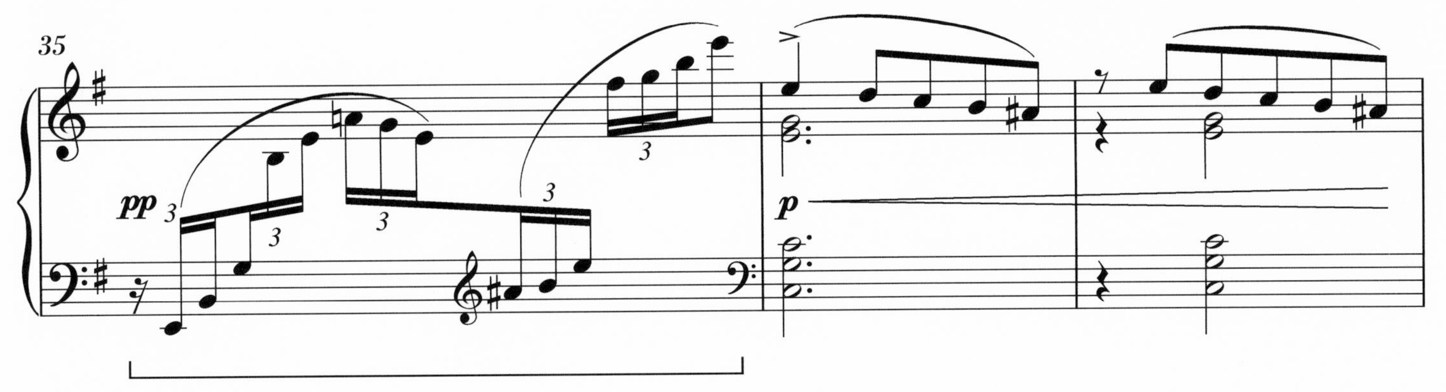
35
pp
p

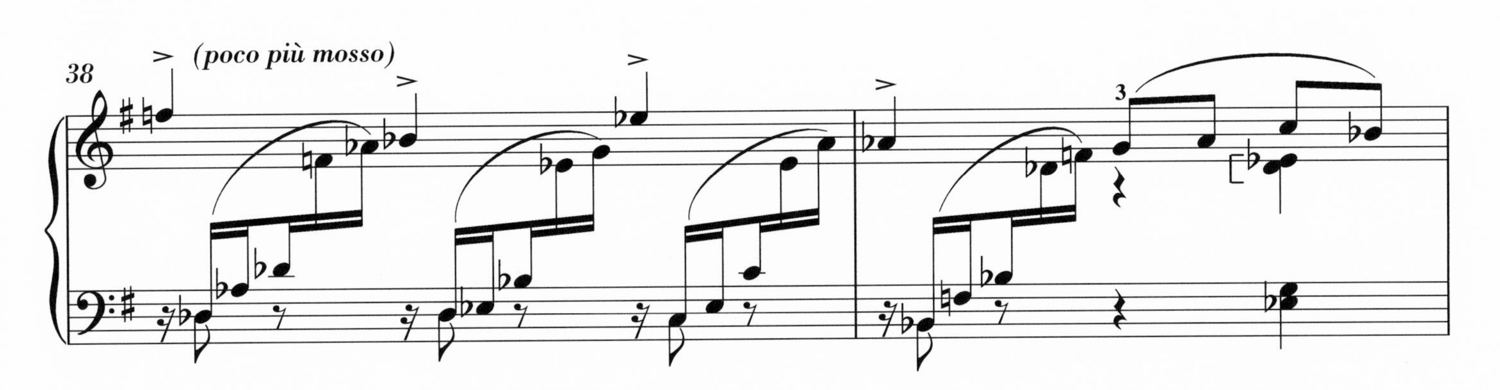
38
(poco più mosso)

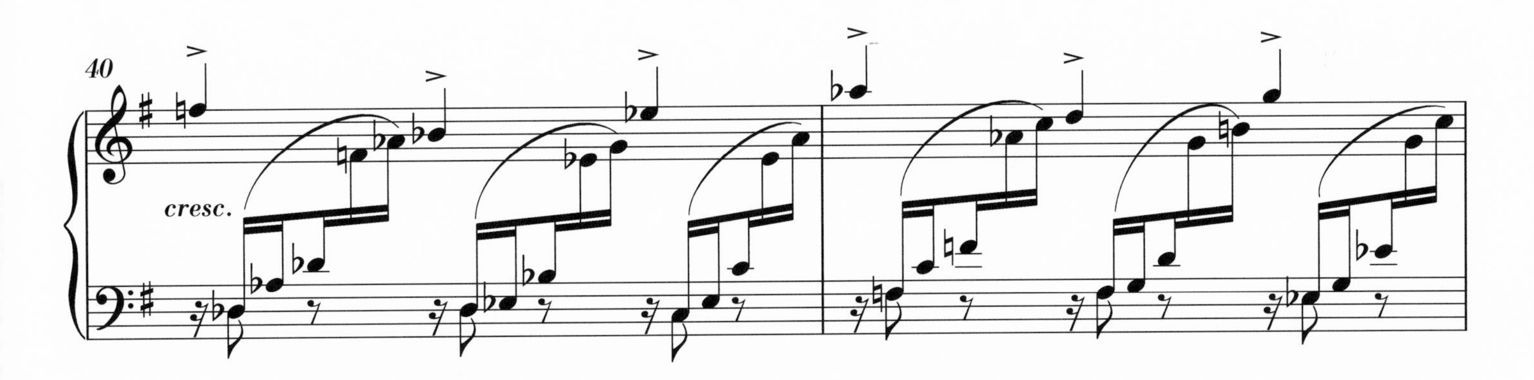
40
cresc.

42
mf

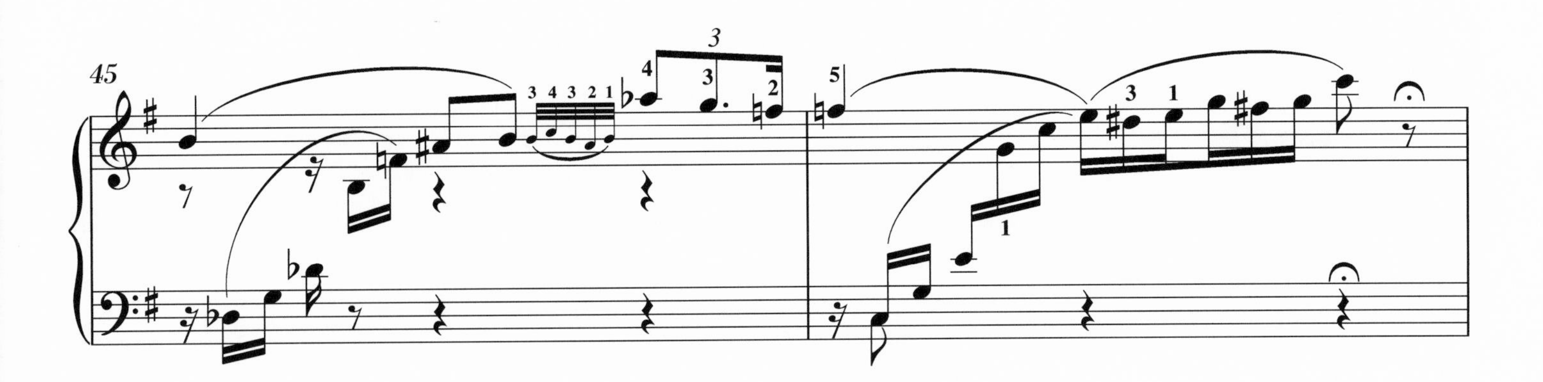
45

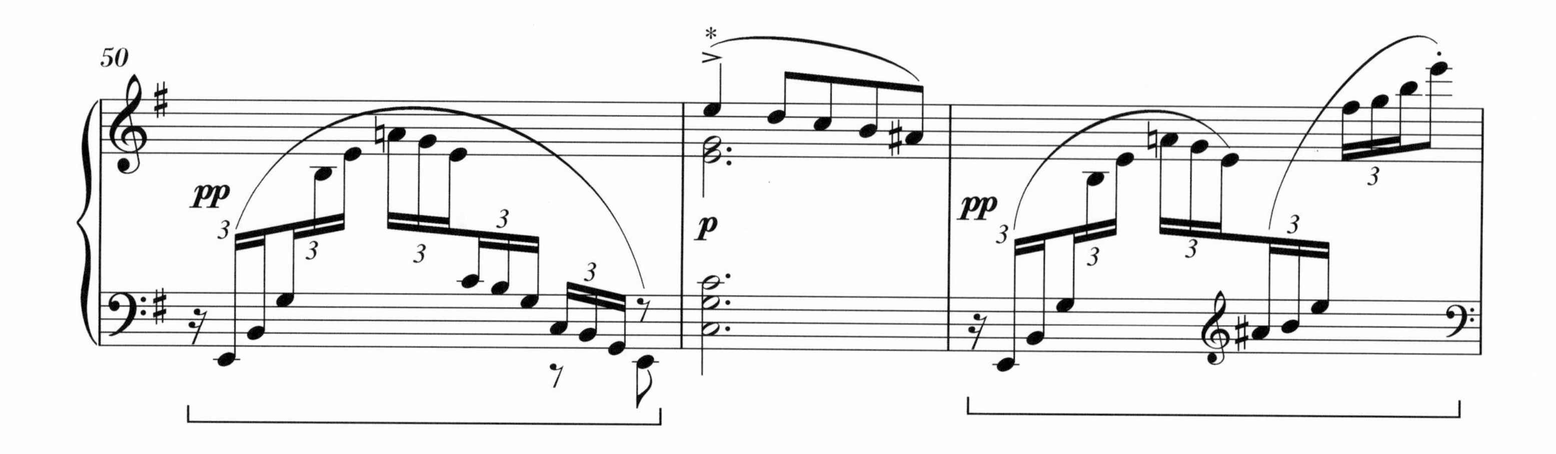

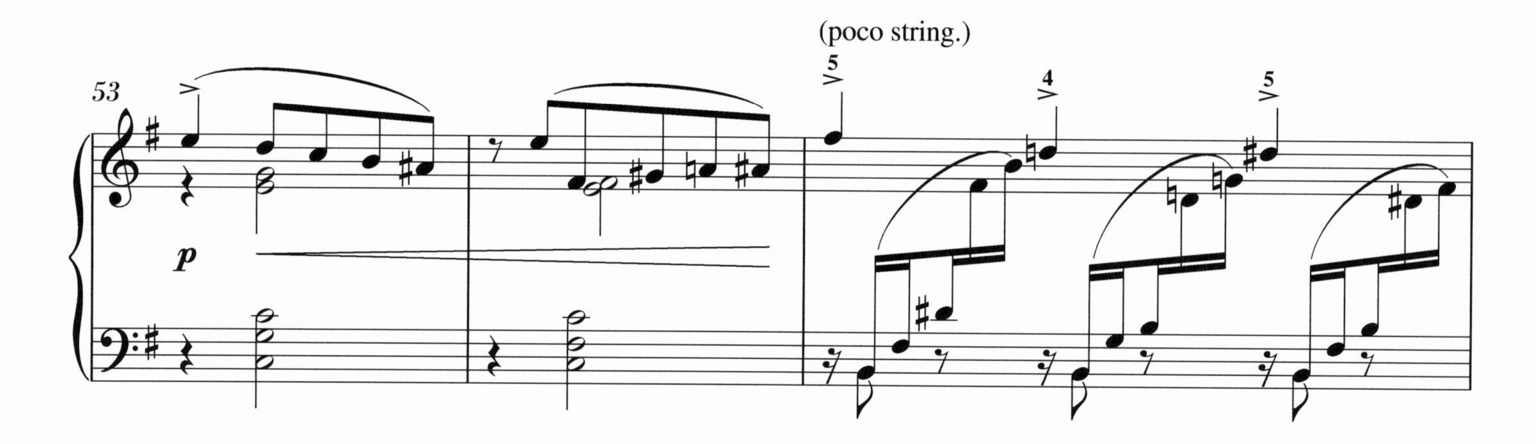

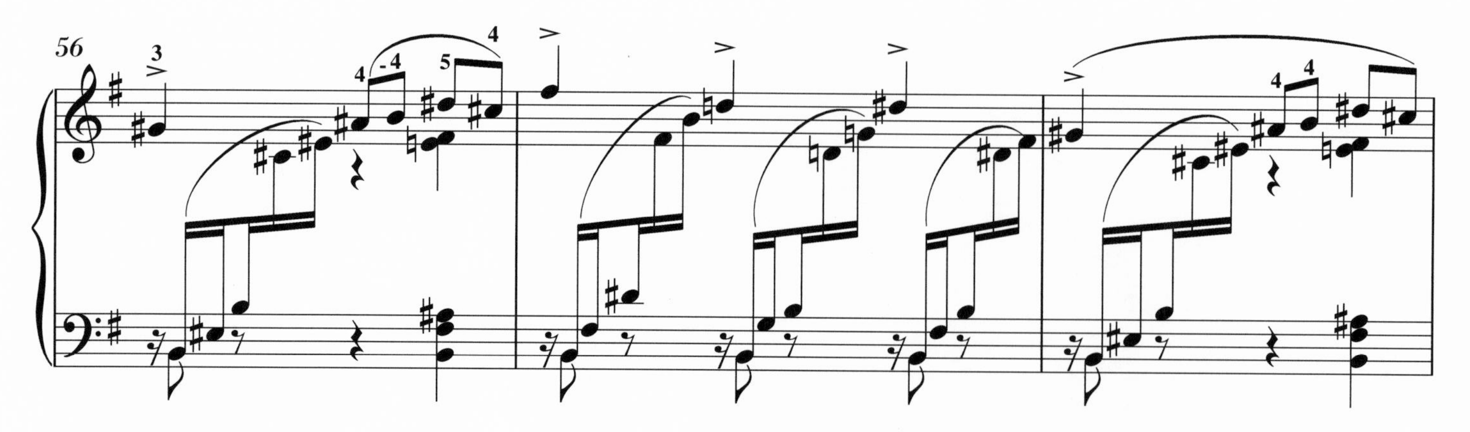

* See Performance Notes

59
dim.

61
riten.
3

(Tempo I)
64
p

68
poco più f

72
p

75

78
poco cresc.

81
mf
dim.

84
p

88
cresc.

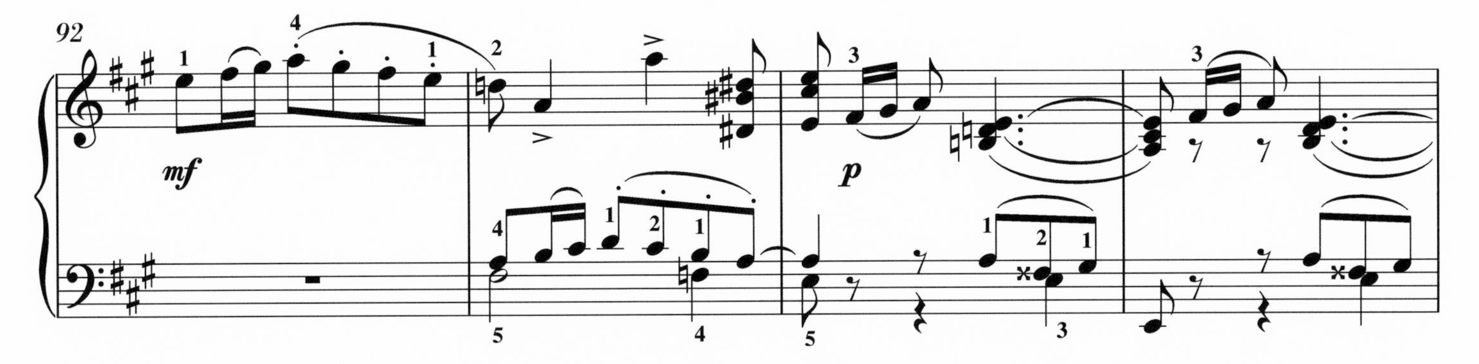
92
mf
p

96
poco riten.
pp

99
ppp

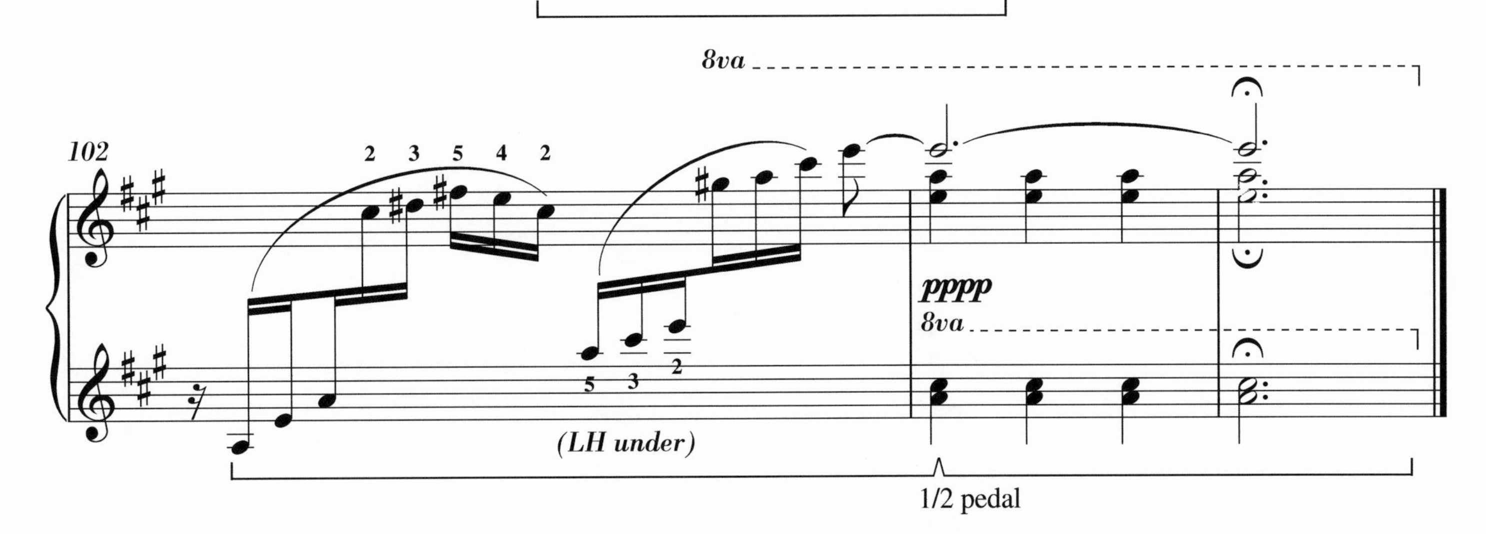
102
8va
pppp
8va
(LH under)
1/2 pedal

February: Carnival
Февраль: Масленица
Fevral’: Maslenitsa

Скоро масленицы бойкой
Закипит широкий пир.
Кн. П. Вяземский

At the lively Mardi Gras
soon a large feast will overflow.
Pyotr Vyazemsky

Pyotr Il’yich Tchaikovsky
Op. 37bis, No. 2

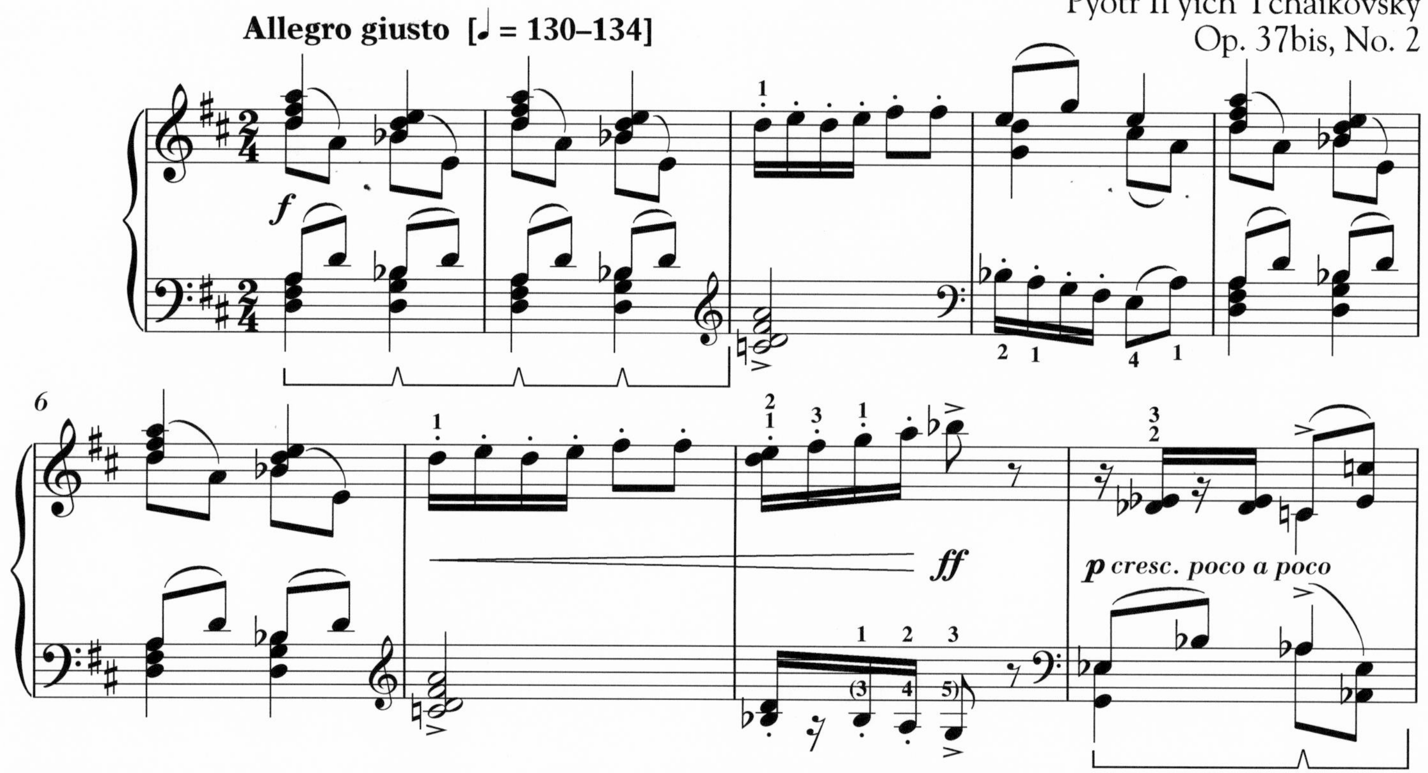

24
f

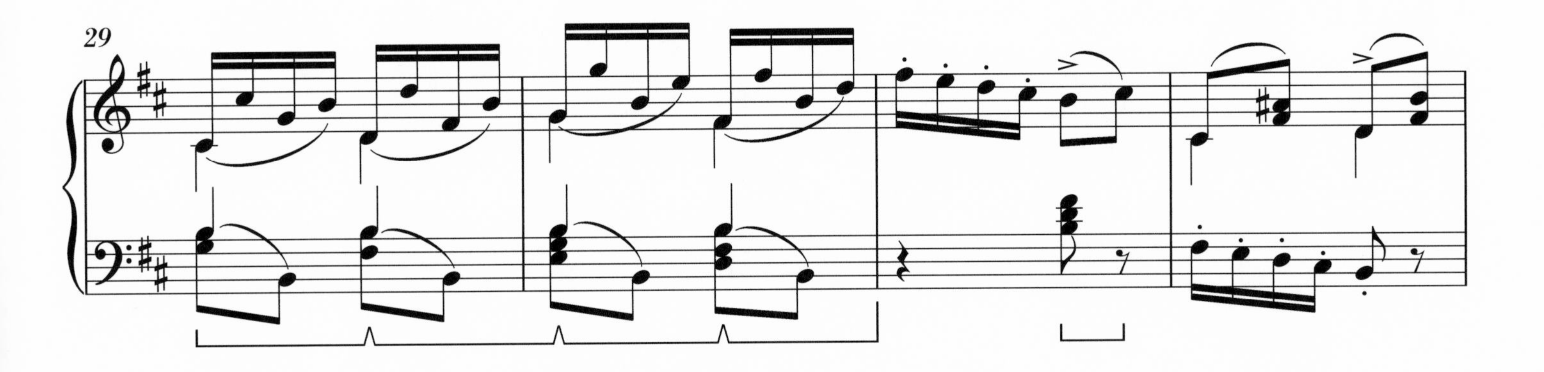
29

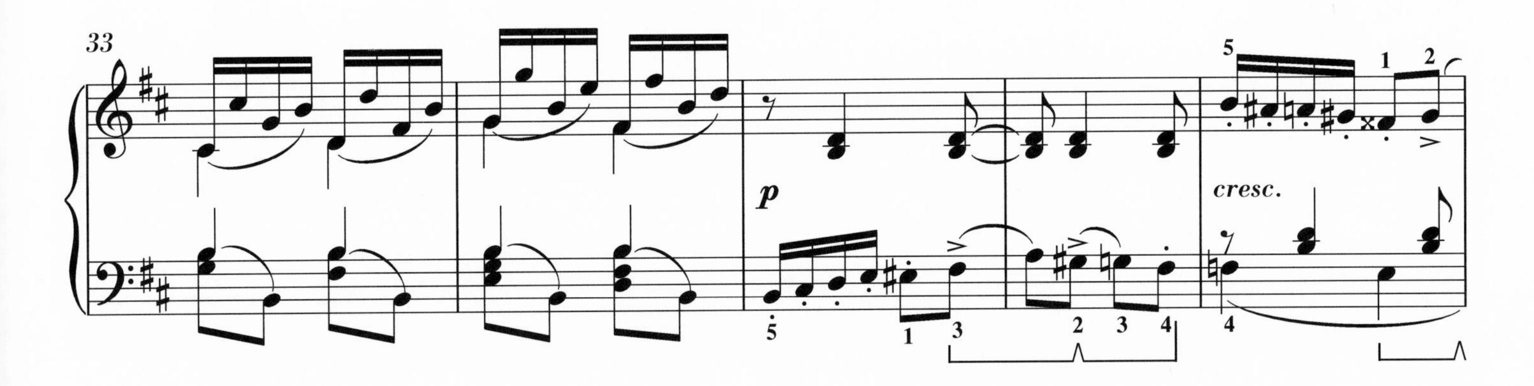
33
p
cresc.

38

43
f

48

53

57
f

61

66
ff
p cresc. poco a poco

71

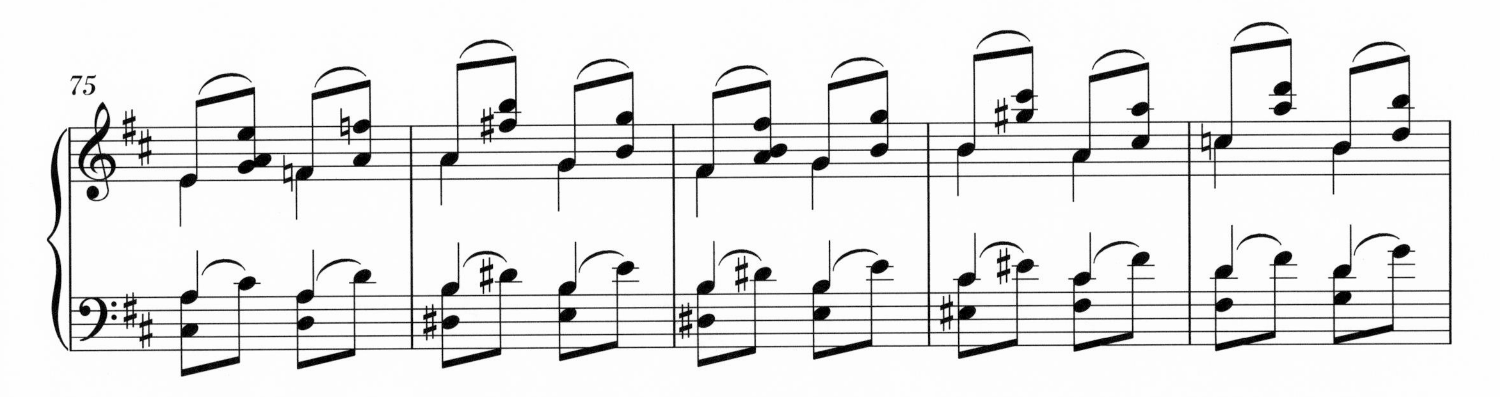
75

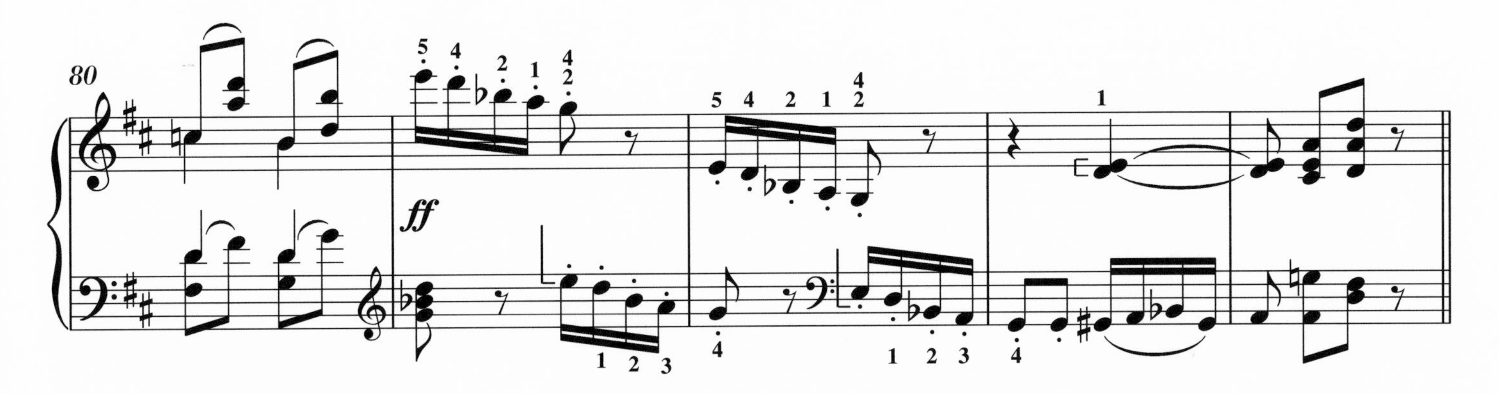
80
ff

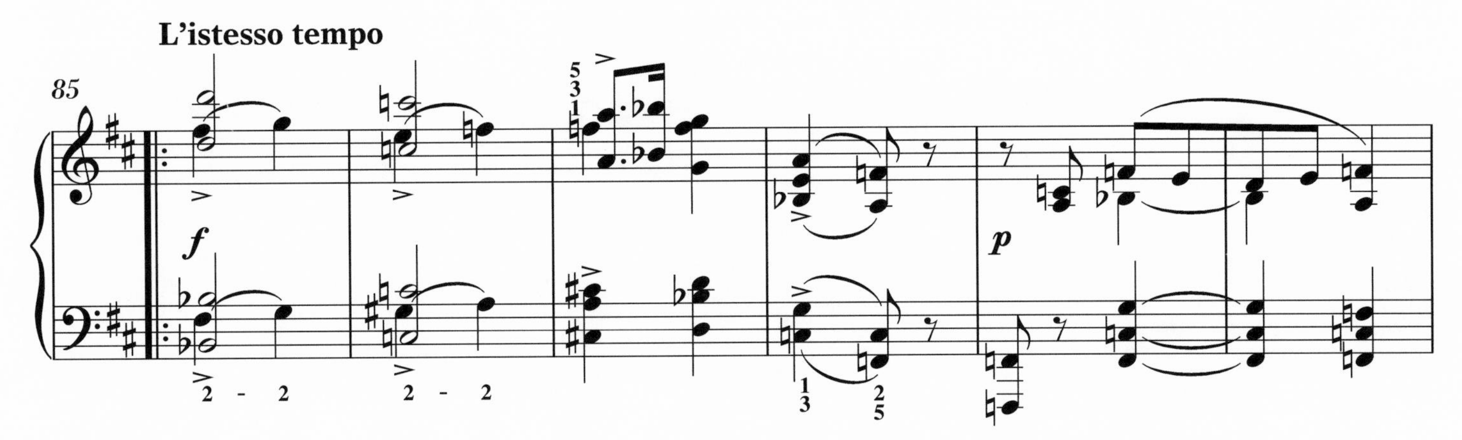
L'istesso tempo
85
f
p

91

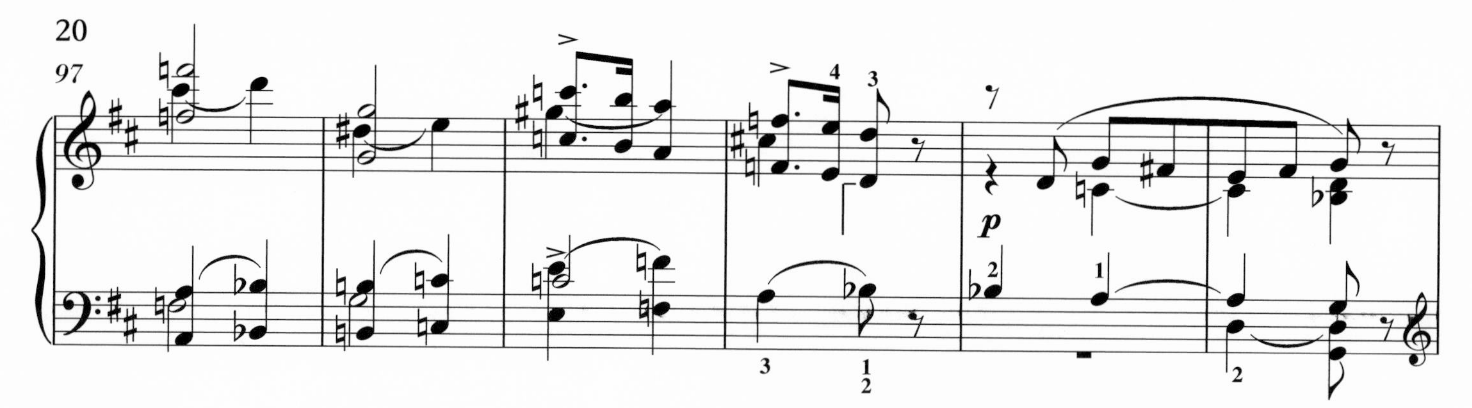

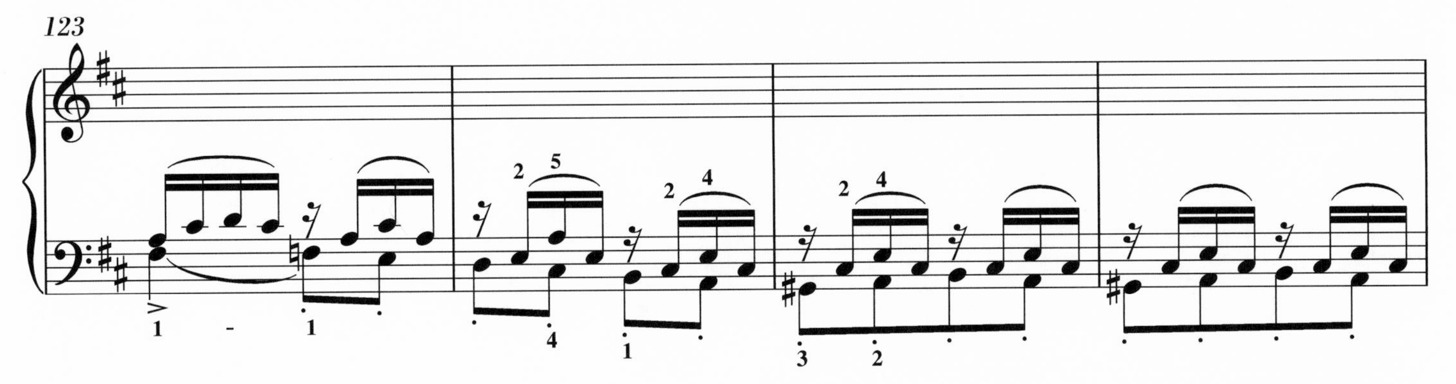
123

127
cresc.

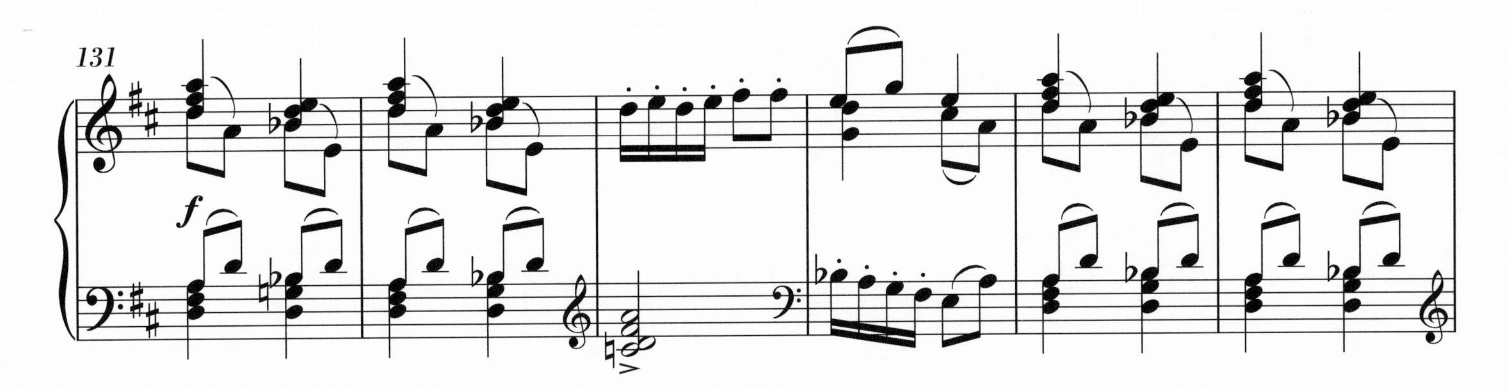
131
f

137
ff
p cresc. poco a poco

141

146

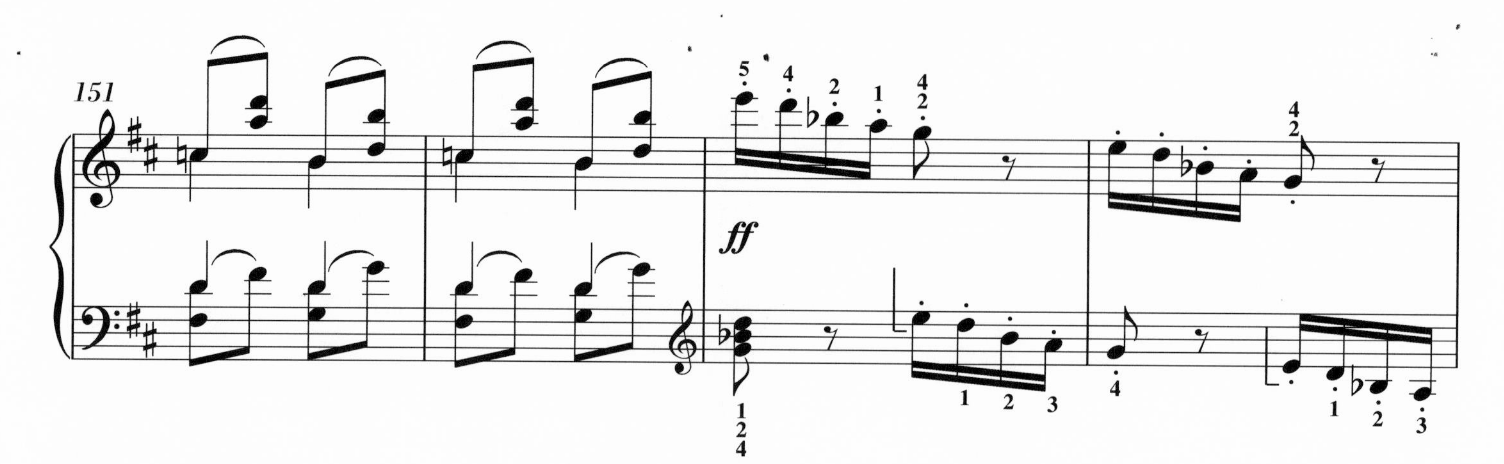
151
ff

155

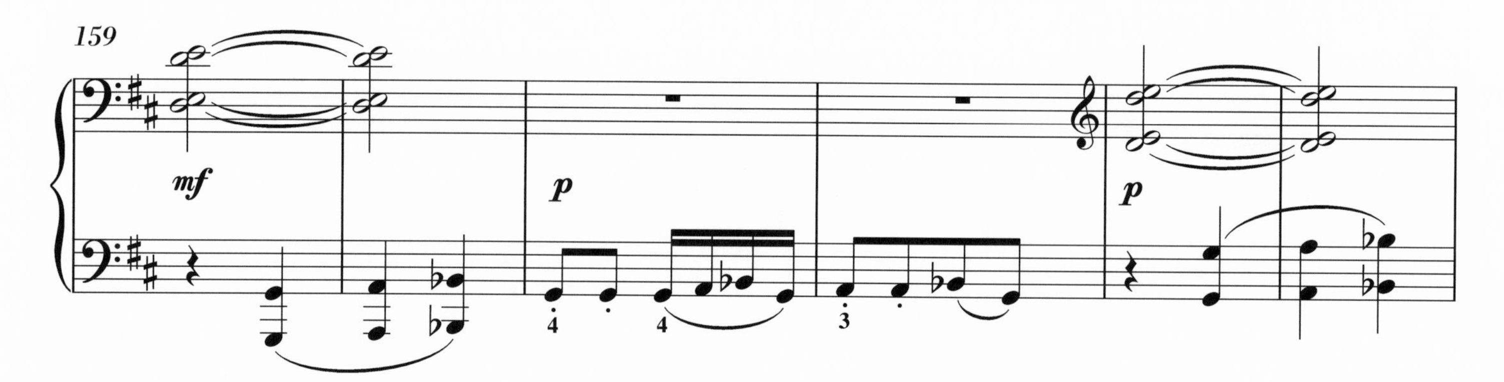
159
mf
p
p

165
pp
fff

March: Song of the Lark
Март: Песнь жаворонка
Mart: Pesn’ zhavoronka

Поле зыблется цветами,
В небе вьются света волны,
Вешних жаворонков пенья
Голубые бездны полны.
А. Майков

The field shimmering with flowers,
the stars swirling in the heavens,
the song of the lark
fills the blue abyss.
Apollon Maykov

Pyotr Il’yich Tchaikovsky
Op. 37bis, No. 3

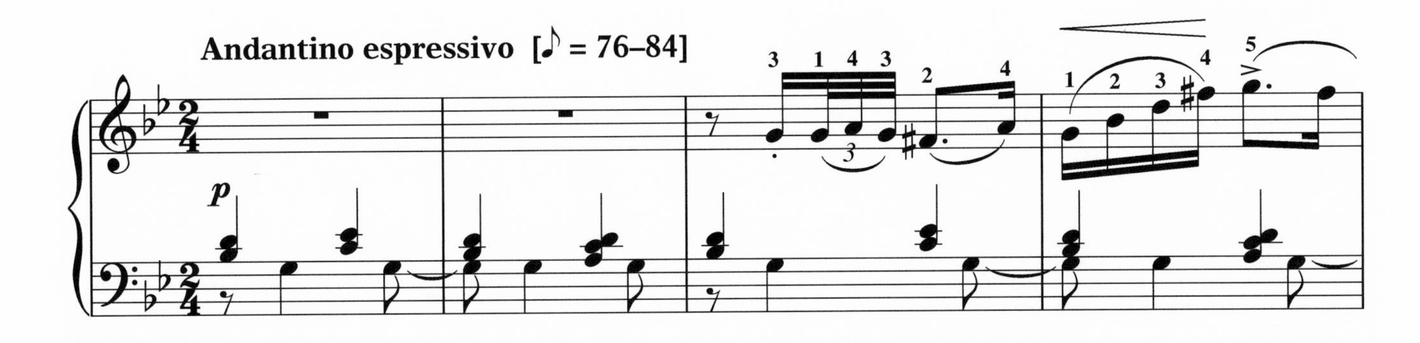

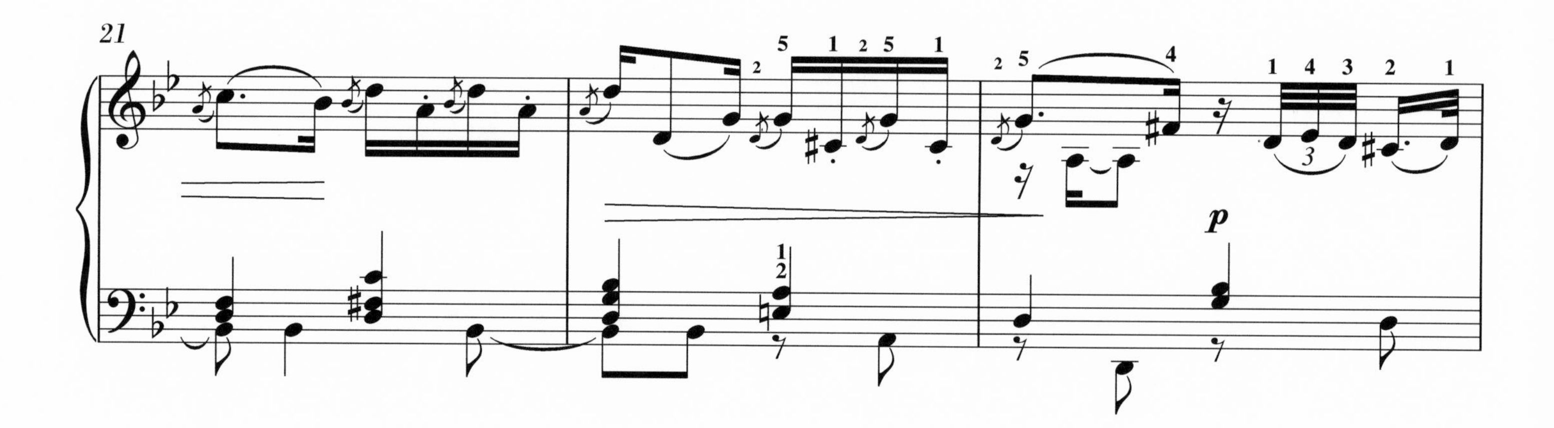
p

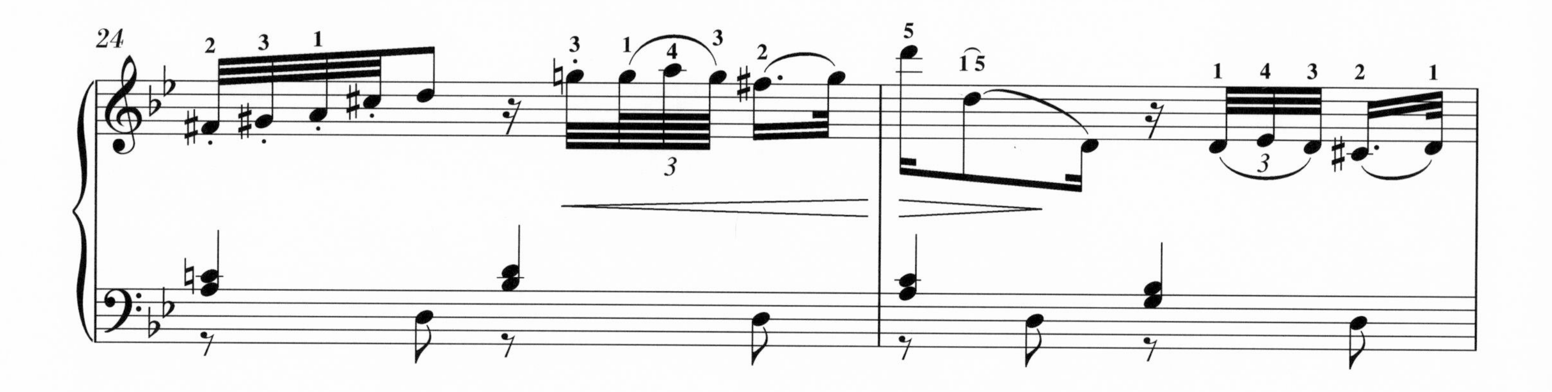

dim.

29
poco ritenuto
a tempo
p

33

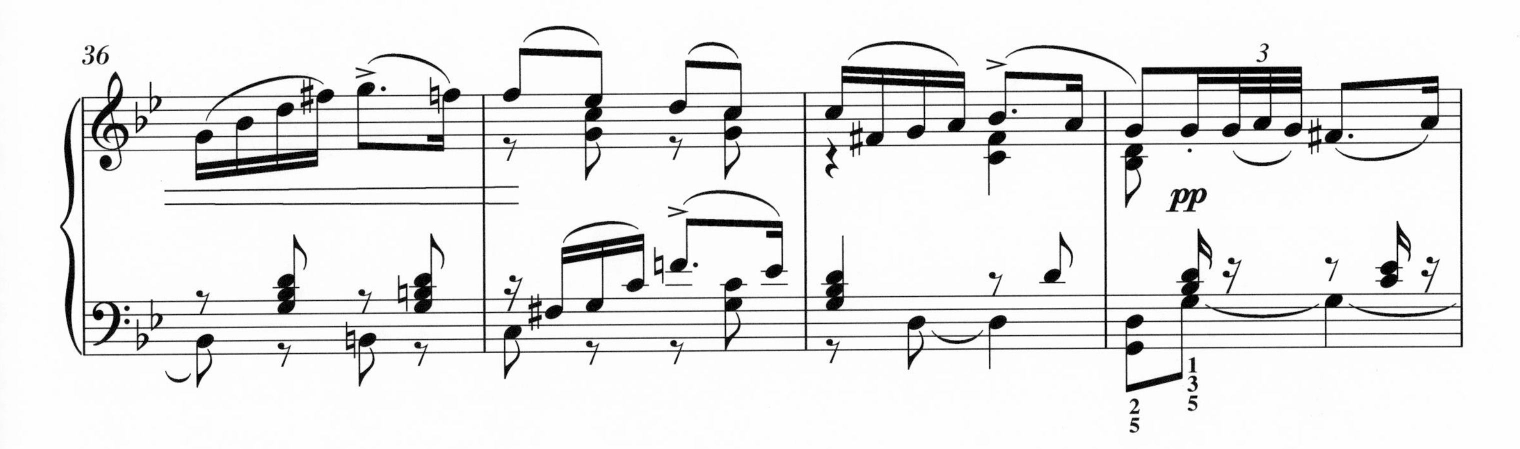
36
pp

40
pp

43
ppp

April: Snowdrop Flower
Апрель: Подснежник
Aprel': Podsnezhnik

Голубенький, чистый
Подснежник-цветок,
А подле сквозистый
Последний снежок.
Последние слёзы
О горе былом
И первые грёзы
О счастье ином...
А. Майков

The blue, pure snowdrop—flower,
and near it the last snowdrops.
The last tears over past griefs,
and first dreams of another happiness.
Apollon Maykov

Pyotr Il'yich Tchaikovsky
Op. 37bis, No. 4

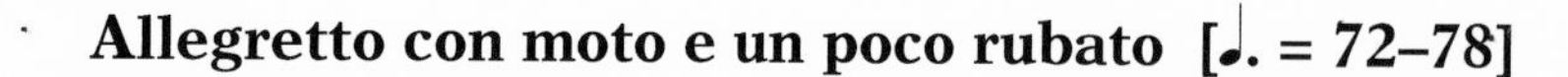

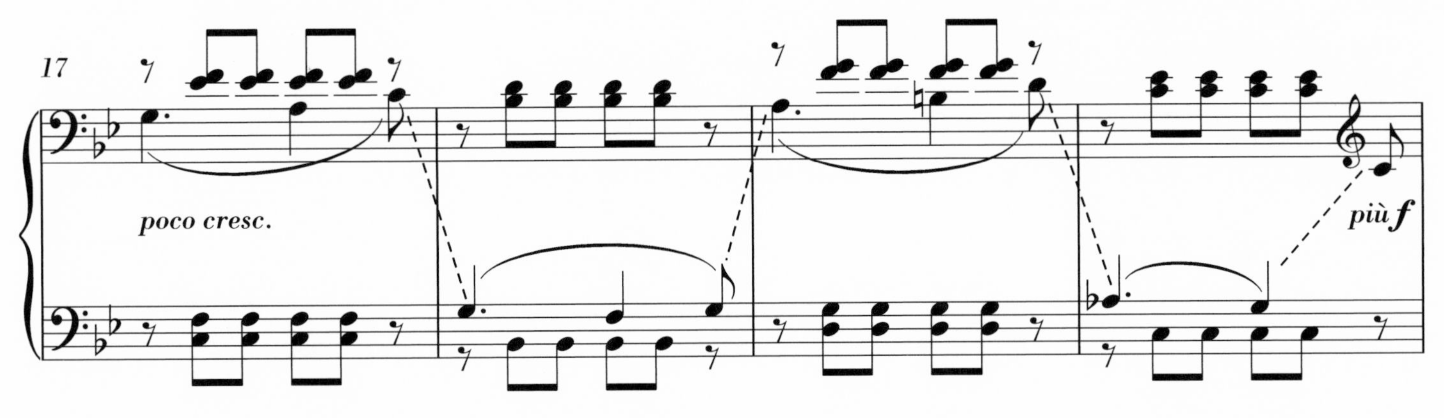
17
poco cresc.
più f

21
p

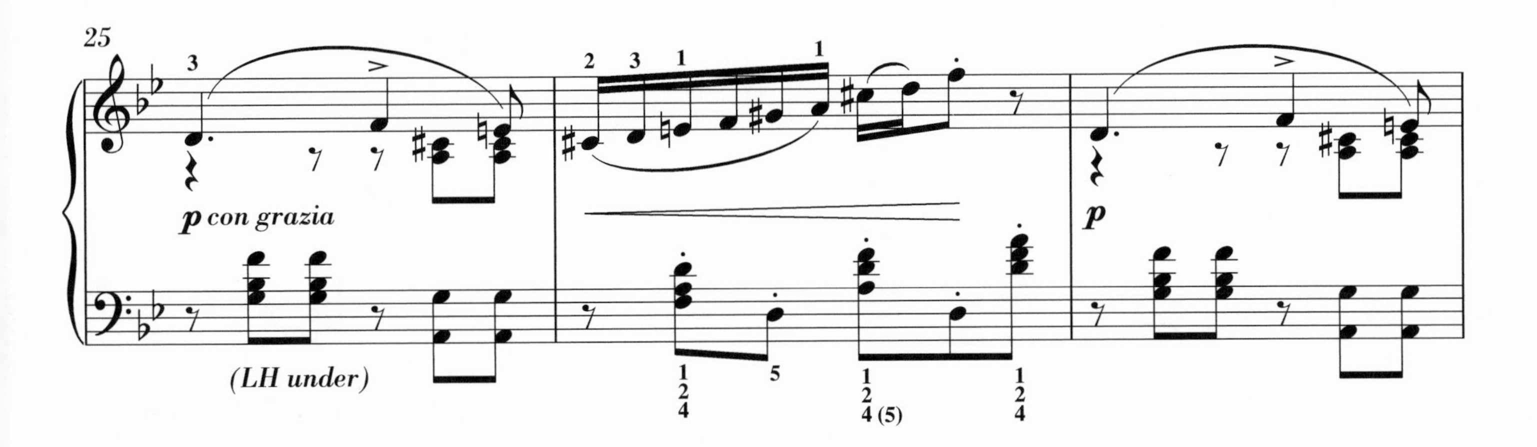
25
p con grazia
(LH under)
p

28
p

31
p
mf

34

38
p

42
p

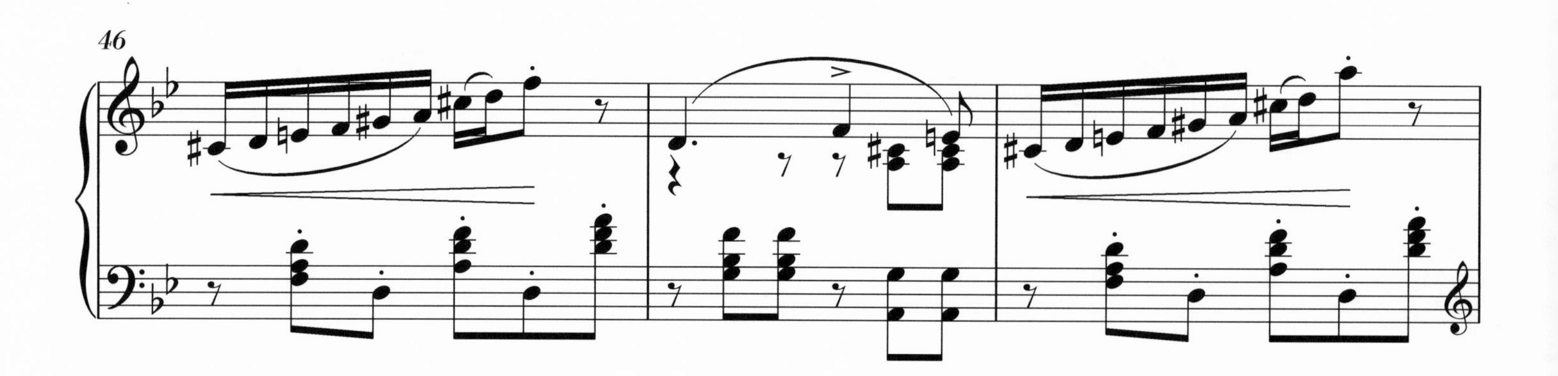
46

49
mf
dim.

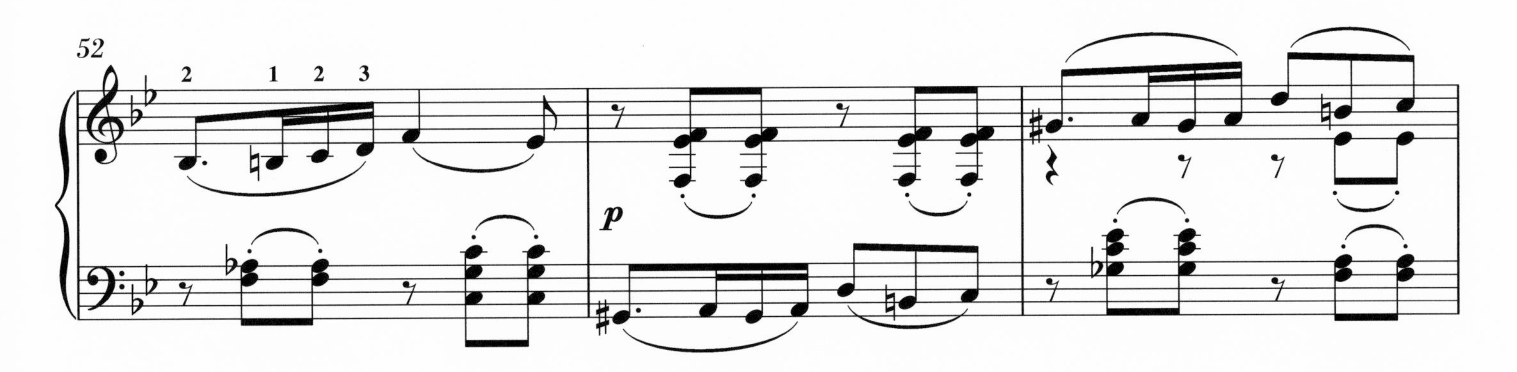
52
p

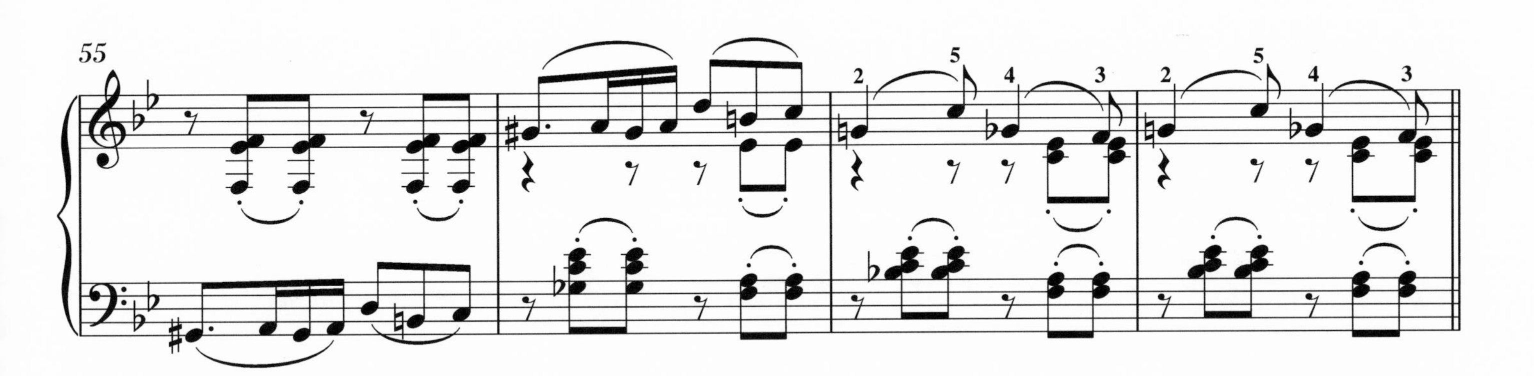
55

59
p dolce
poco cresc.

63
mf
p

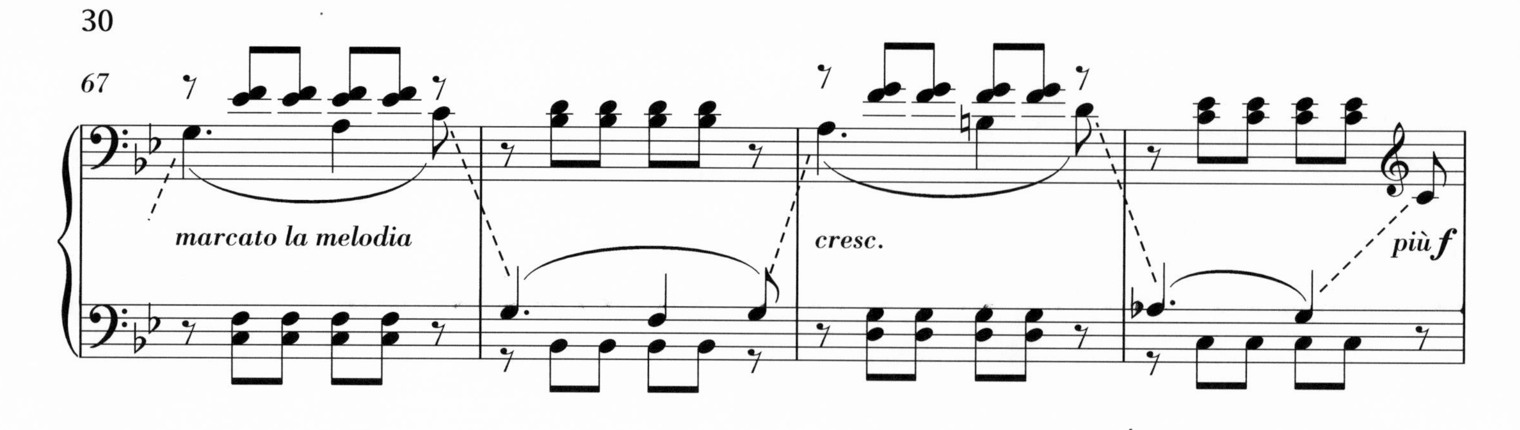
67
marcato la melodia
cresc.
più f

71
dim.

75
pp

79
morendo si poco a poco

83
(ad libitum)
ppp

May: White Nights
Май: Белые Ночи
Mai: Belye Nochi

Какая ночь! На всем какая нега!
Благодарю родной полночный край!
Из царства льдов, из царства вьюг и снега
Как свеж и чист твой вылетает май.
А. Фет

What a night! What bliss all about!
I thank my native north country!
From the kingdom of ice,
snowstorms and snow,
how fresh and clean May flies in!
Afanasy Fet

Pyotr Il'yich Tchaikovsky
Op. 37bis, No. 5

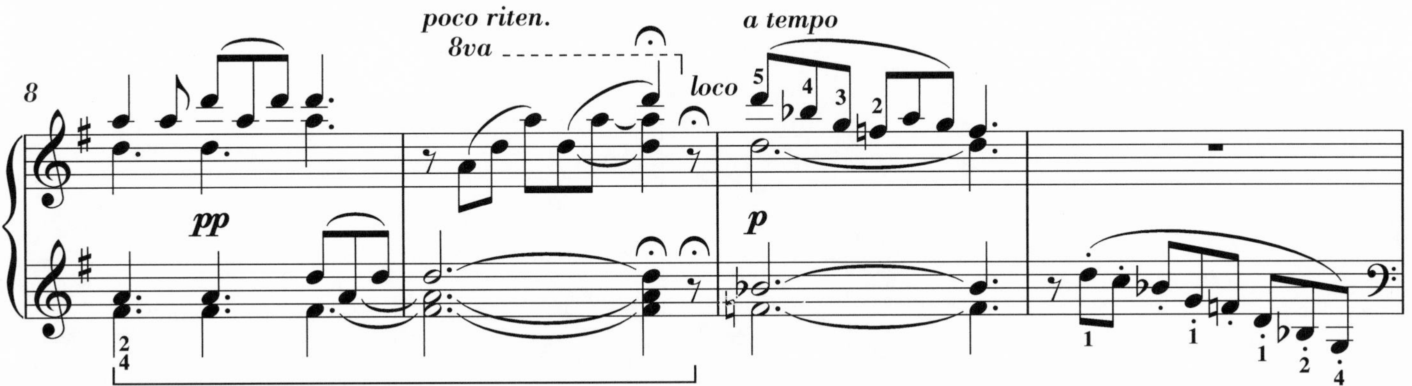

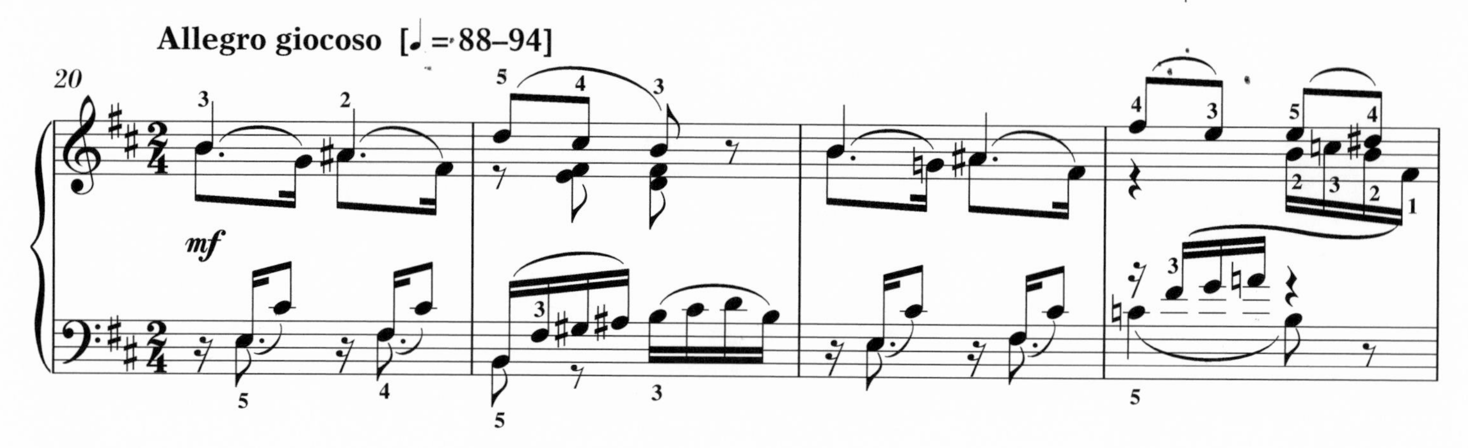

* See Performance Notes

36

40
(poco ritard.)
cresc.

poco meno mosso
44
f

48
dim.

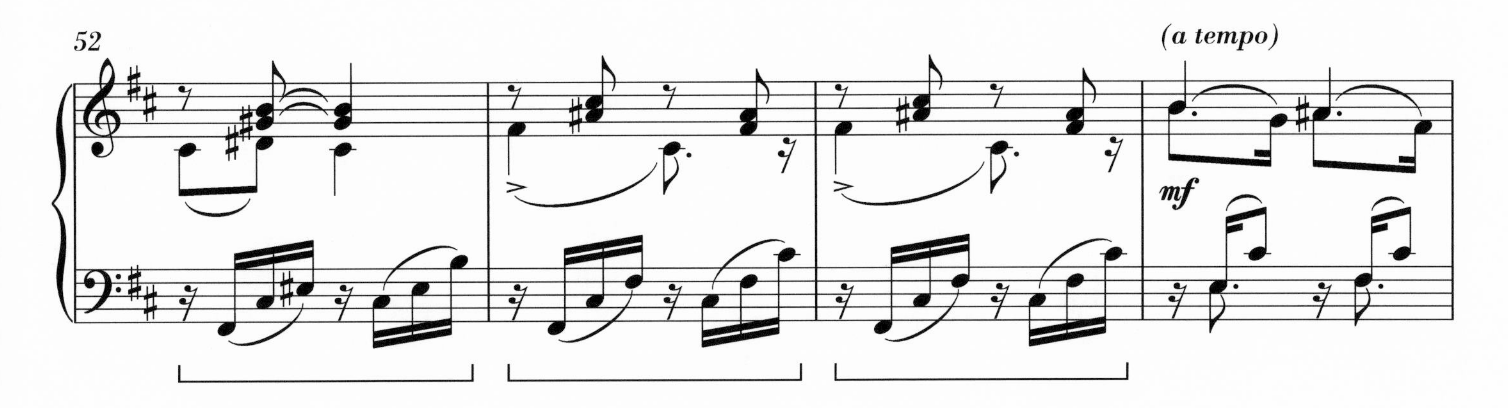
(a tempo)
52
mf

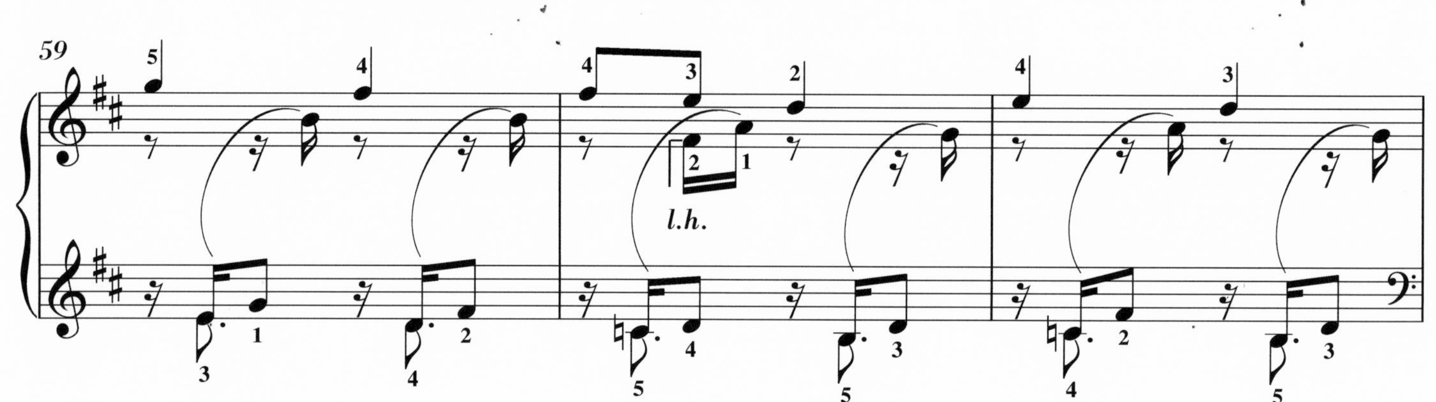
l.h.

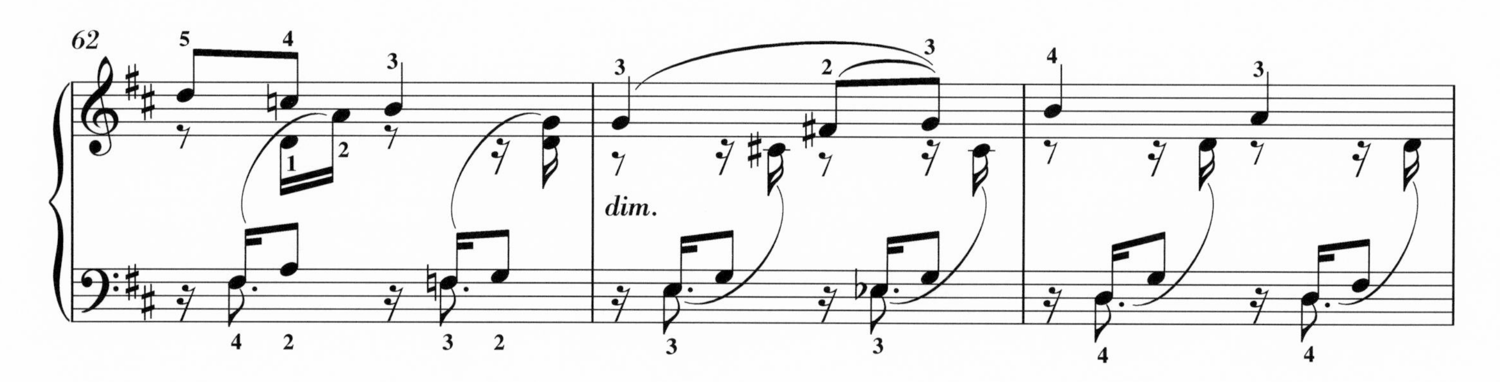
dim.

ritard.
p

Andantino
p

71
poco cresc.

poco riten.
8va
a tempo
75
pp
p

78

81
p espress.

85
pp
ppp

June: Barcarole
Июнь: Баркарола
Iiun’: Barkarola

Выйдем на берег, там волны
Ноги нам будут лобзать,
Звёзды с таинственной грустью
Будут над нами сиять.
А. Плещеев

Let us go to the shore;
There the waves will kiss our legs.
With mysterious sadness
The stars will shine down on us.
Aleksey Pleshcheyev

Pyotr Il’yich Tchaikovsky
Op. 37bis, No. 6

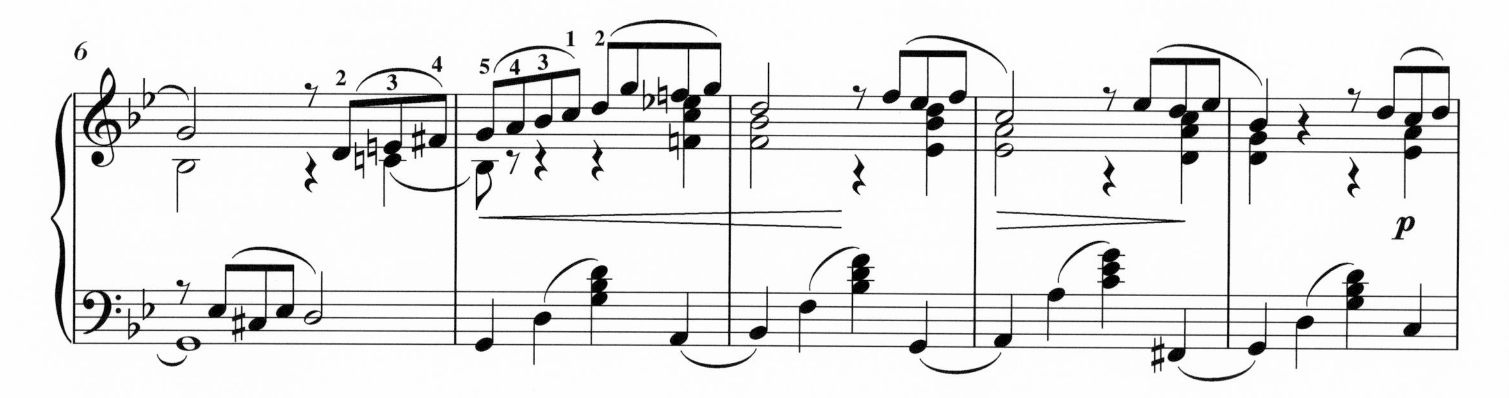

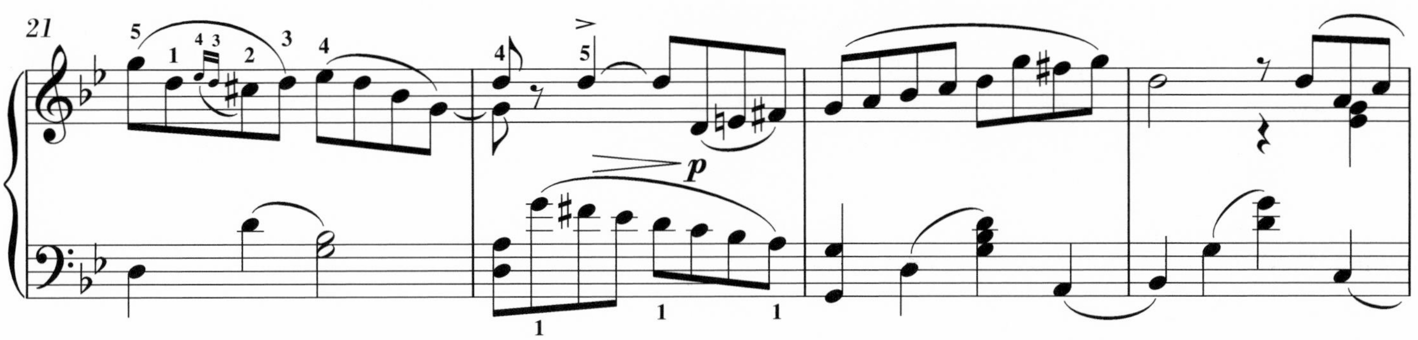

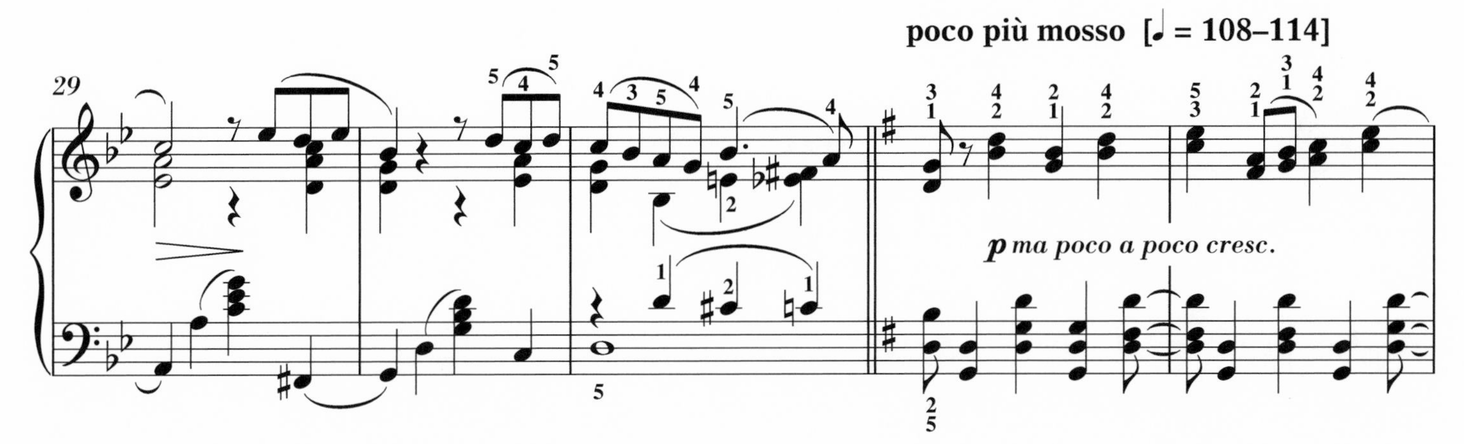

* Some editions have "Allegro giocoso" here. This is not in the autograph.

44
cresc.

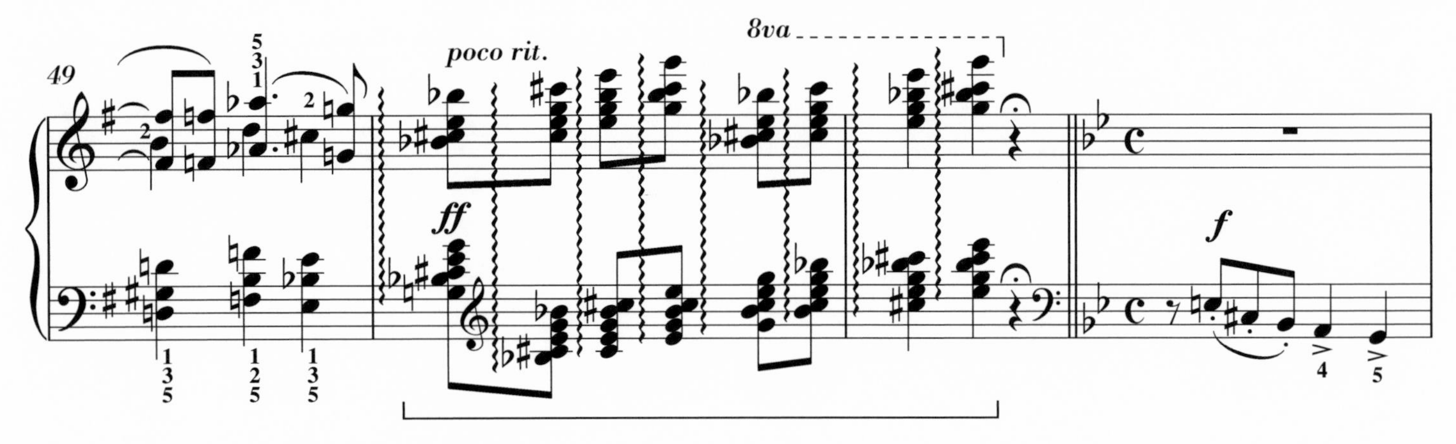
49
poco rit.
8va
ff
f

53
Tempo I
f
p

57

61
poco più f

65

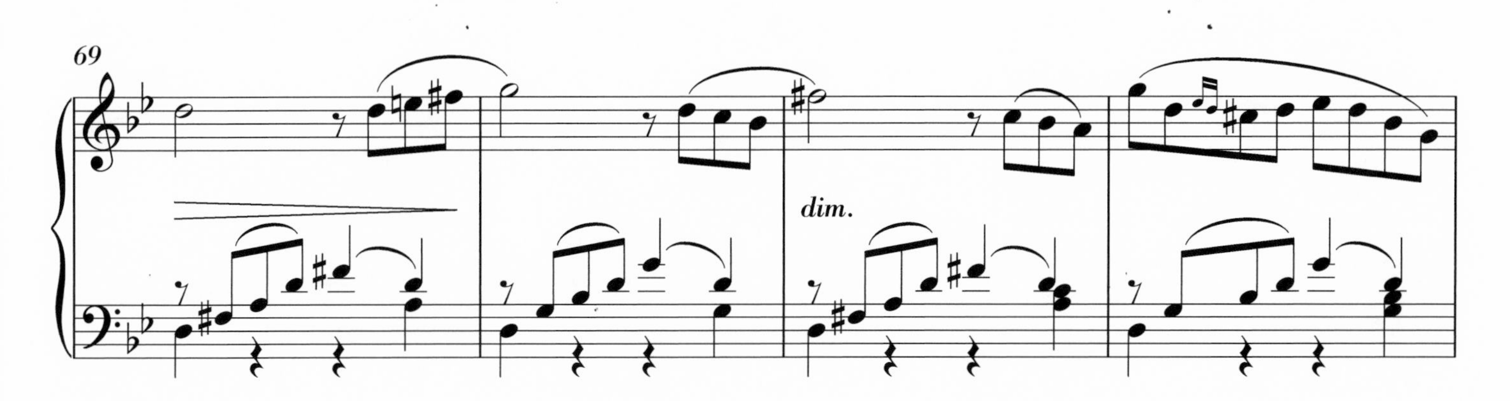
69
dim.

73
p

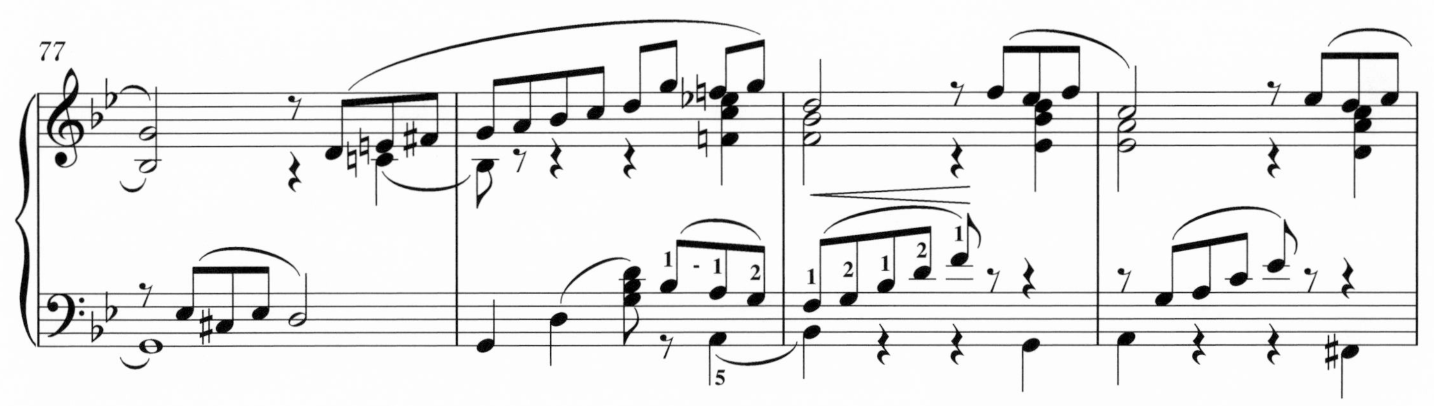
77

81
p

* Some editions have an octave on the second beat. The autograph has a fifth.

July: Song of the Reaper
Июль: Песнь Косаря
Iiul': Pesn' kosaria

Раззудись, плечо,
Размахнись, рука!
Ты пахни в лицо,
Ветер с полудня!
А. Кольцов

Move the shoulders,
shake the arms!
And the noon wind
breathes in the face!
Aleksey Koltsov

Pyotr Il'yich Tchaikovsky
Op. 37bis, No. 7

Allegro moderato con moto [𝅗𝅥 = 62–68]

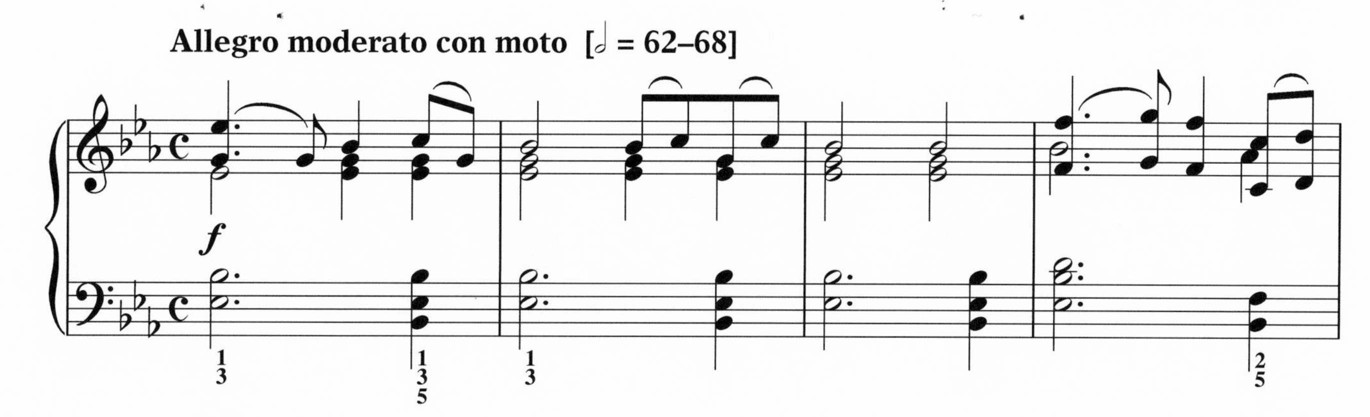

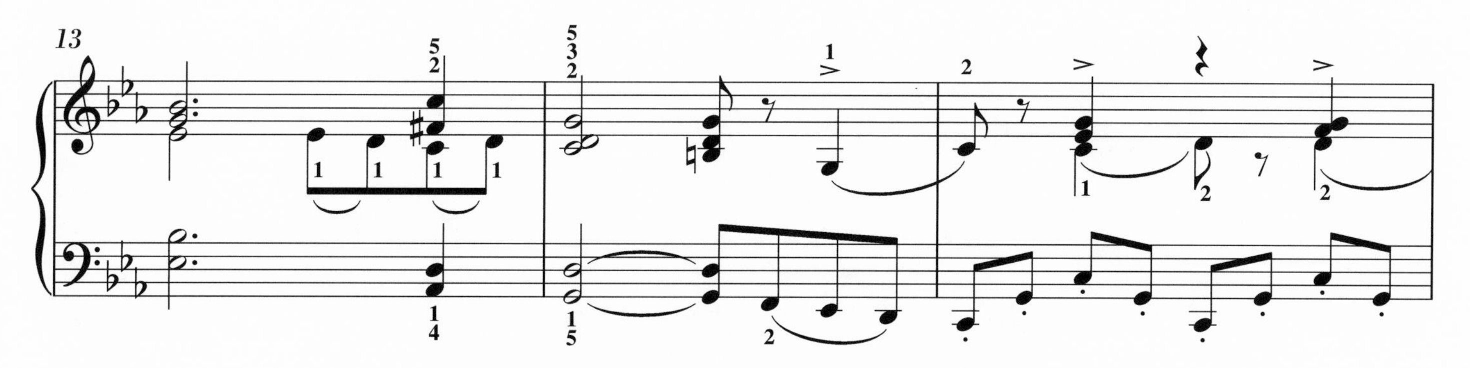

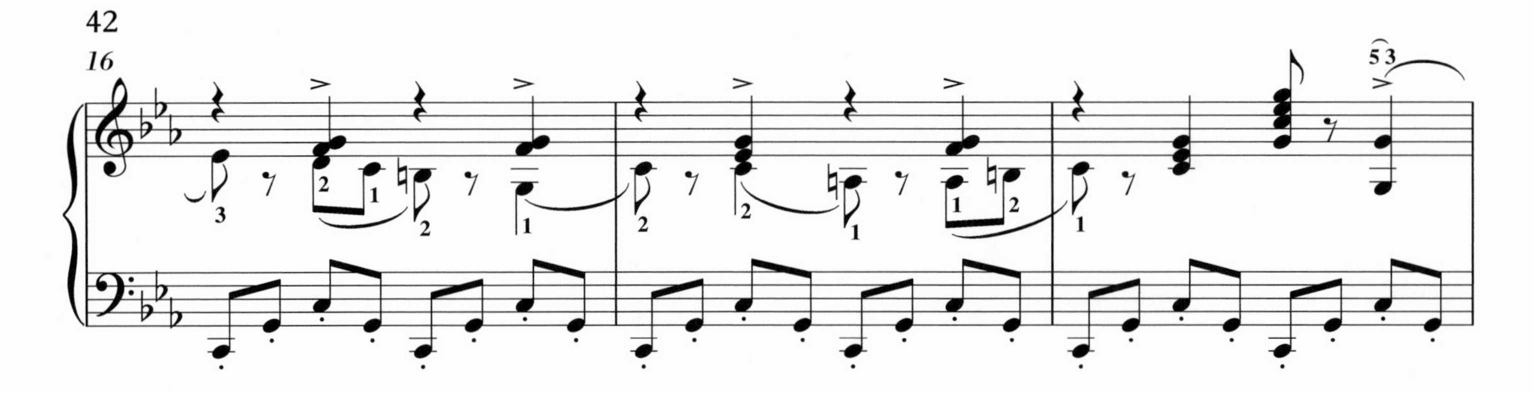

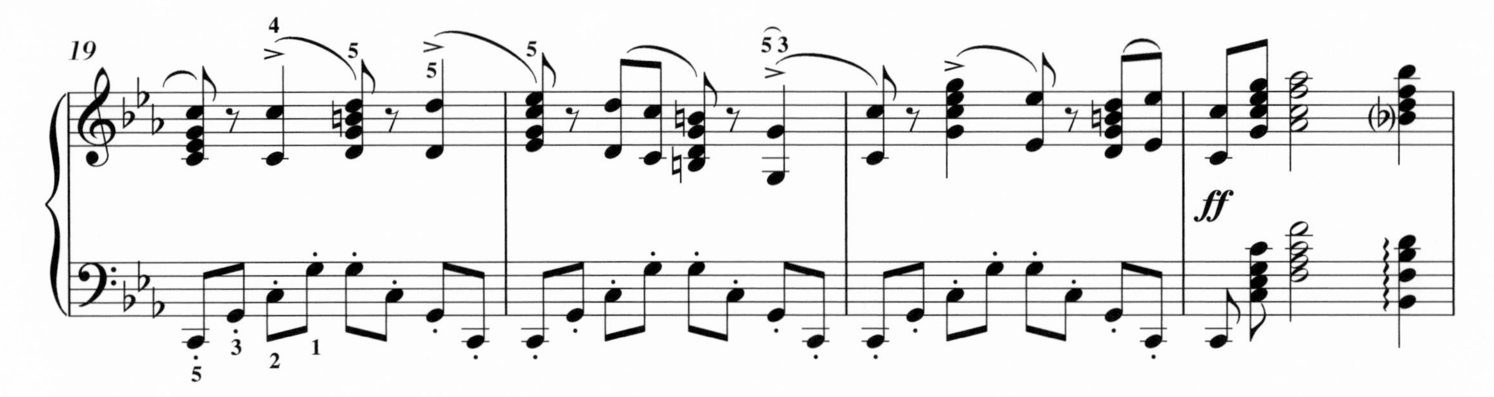

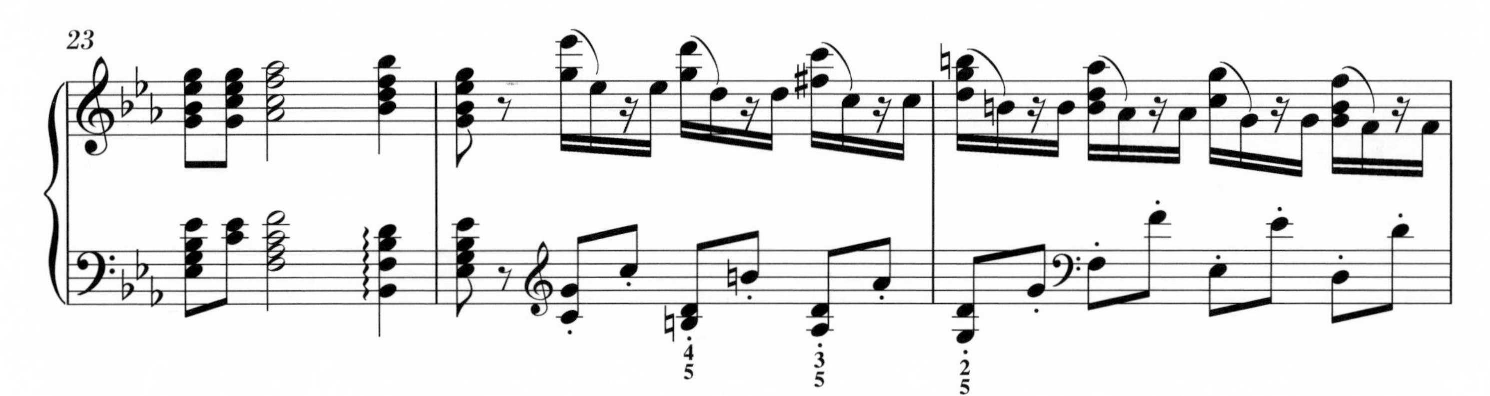

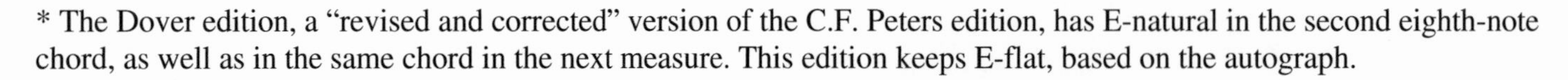
* The Dover edition, a “revised and corrected” version of the C.F. Peters edition, has E-natural in the second eighth-note chord, as well as in the same chord in the next measure. This edition keeps E-flat, based on the autograph.

poco diminuendo

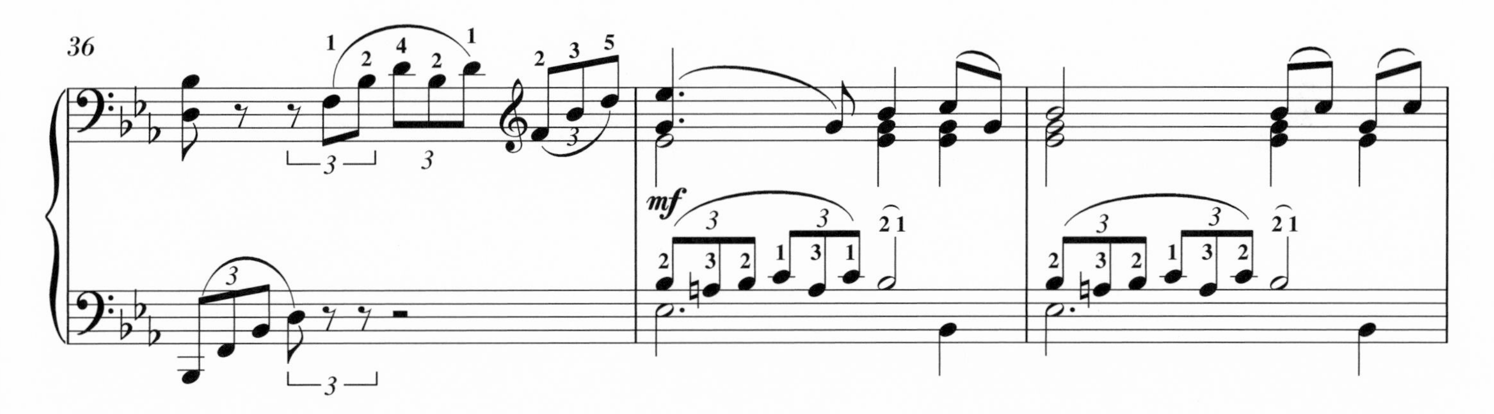
mf

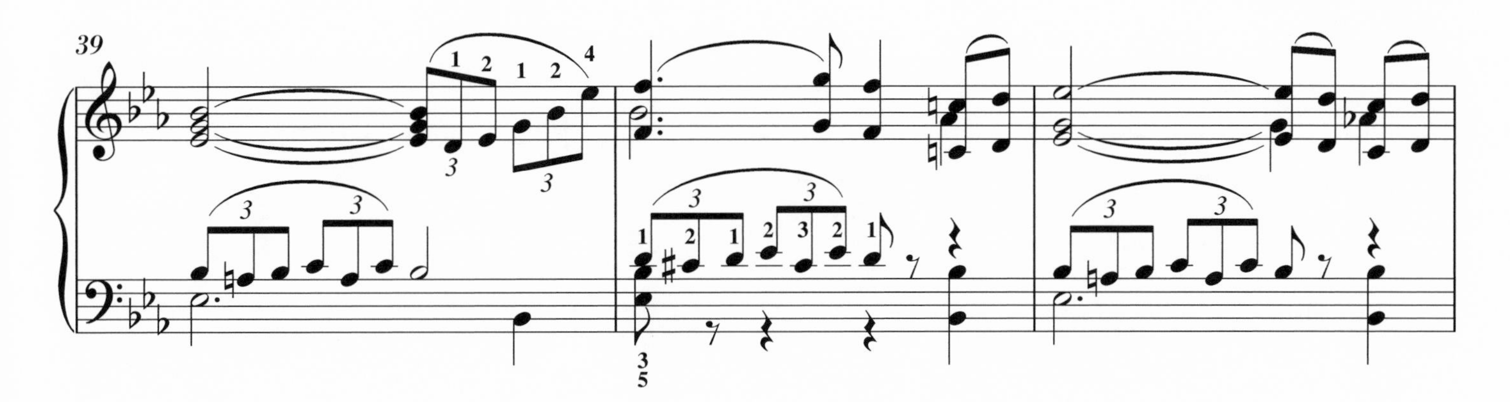

45

48
poco a poco diminuendo

51

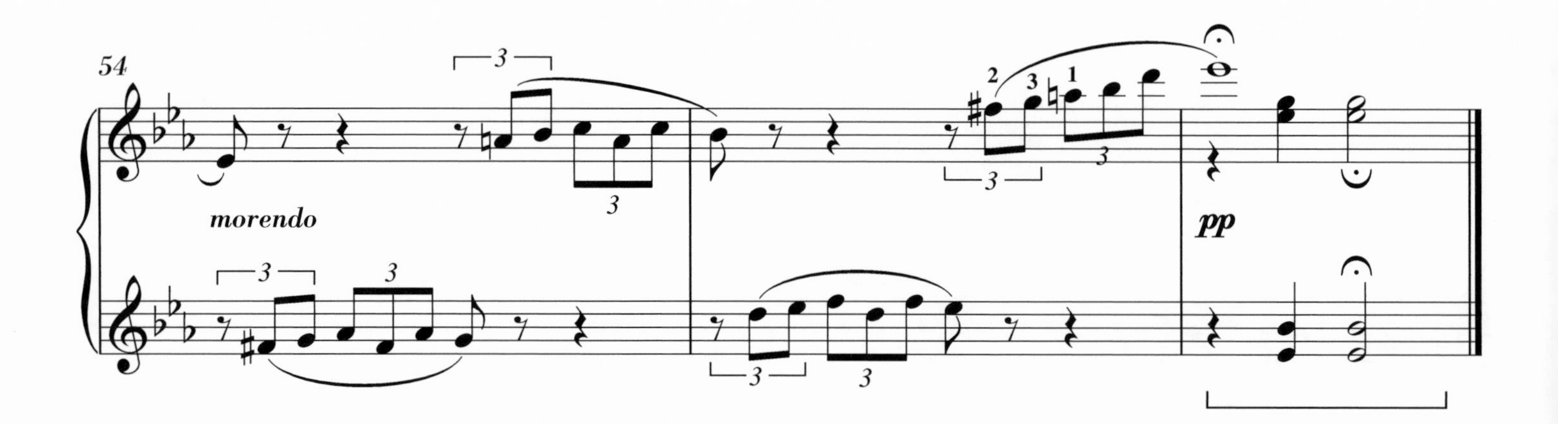
54
morendo
pp

August: Scherzo (Harvest)
Август: Жатва
Avgust: Zhatva

Люди семьями
Принялися жать,
Косить под корень
Рожь высокую!
В копны частые
Снопы сложены,
От возов всю ночь
Скрыпит музыка.
А. Кольцов

The harvest has grown,
people in families
cutting the tall rye
down to the root!
Put together the haystacks,
music screeching all night
from the hauling carts.
Aleksey Koltsov

Pyotr Il'yich Tchaikovsky
Op. 37bis, No. 8

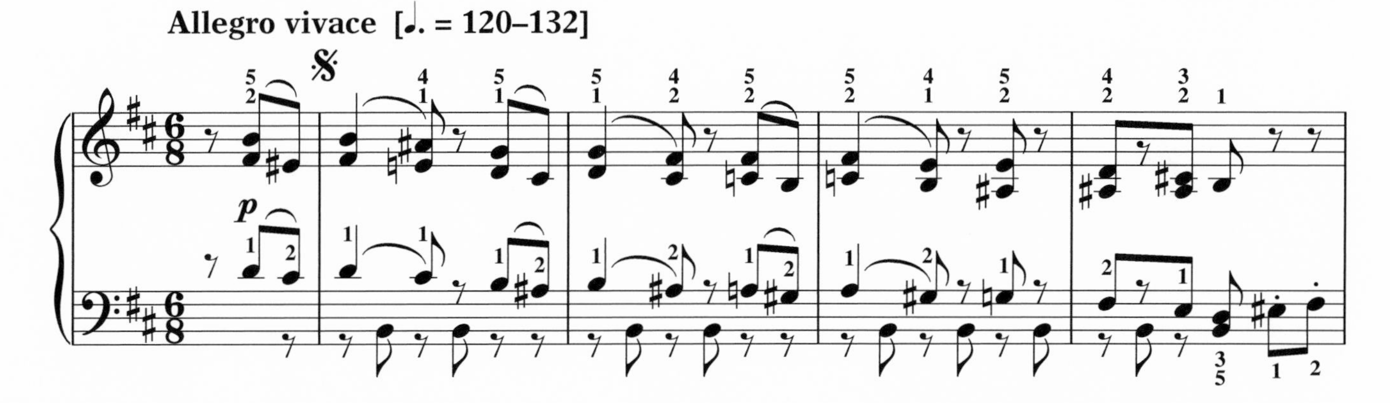

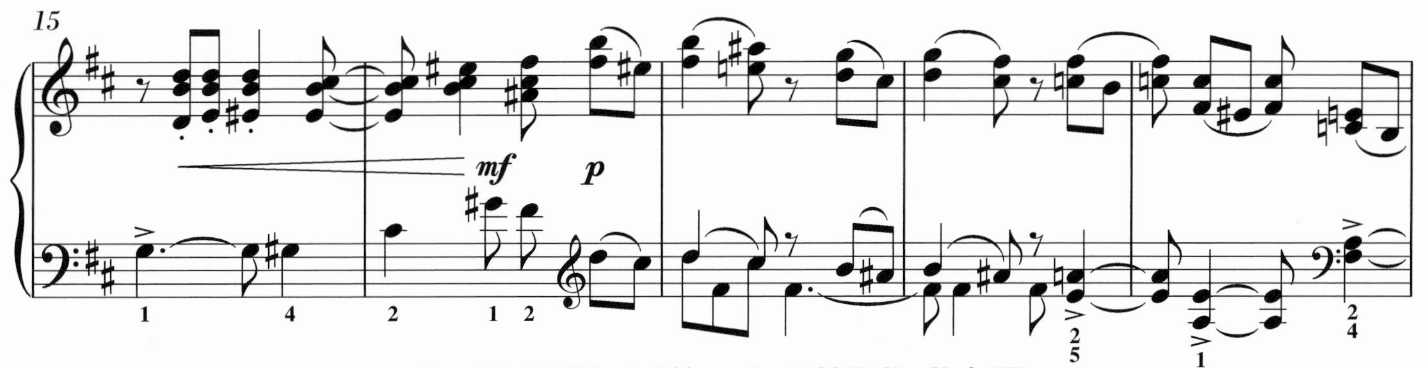

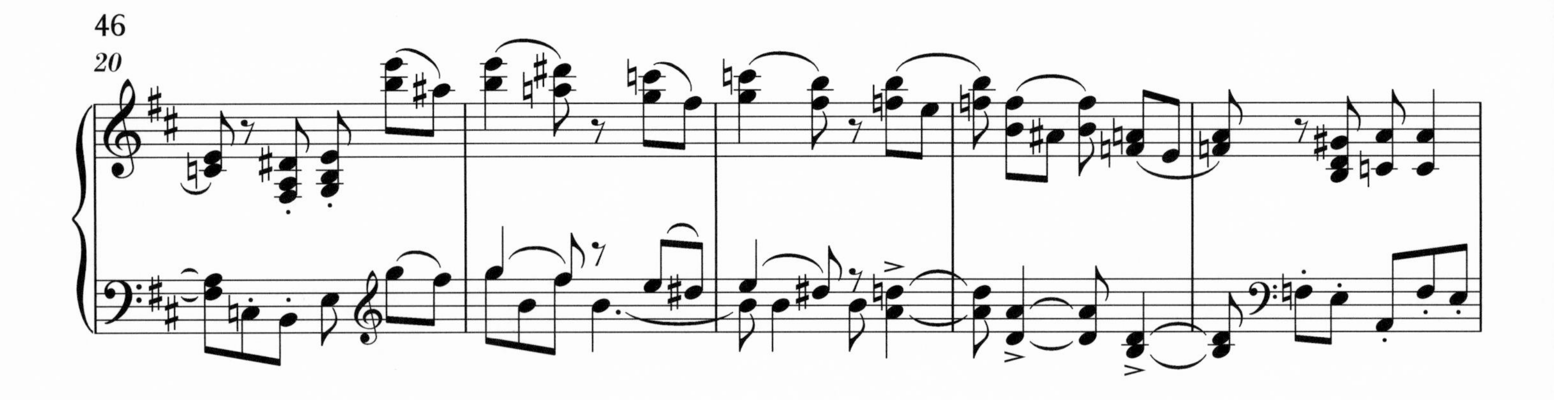
20

25
cresc.

30
f

35
p

40
poco

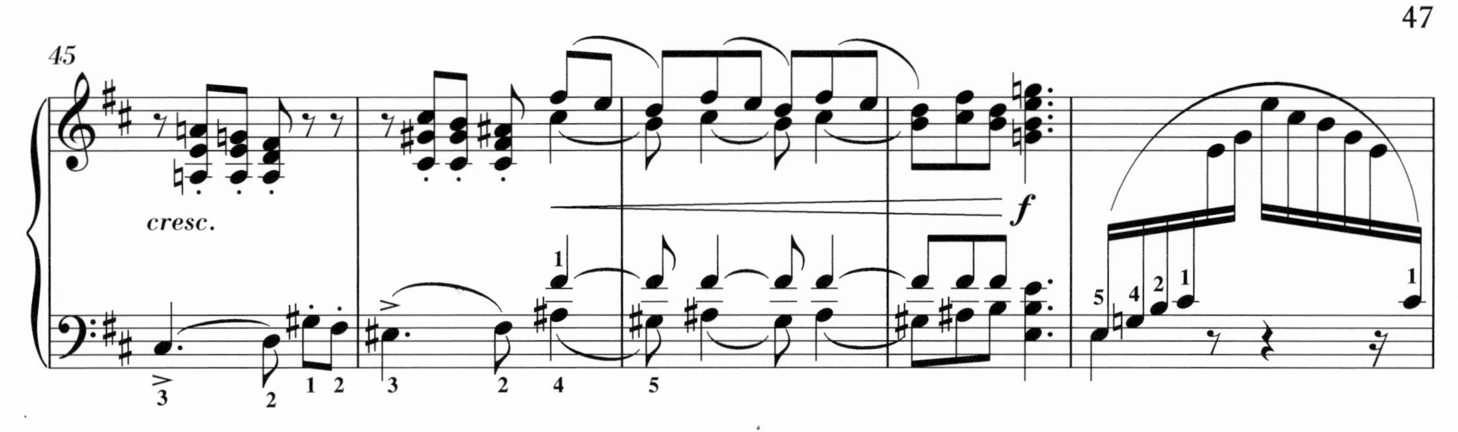
45
cresc.
f

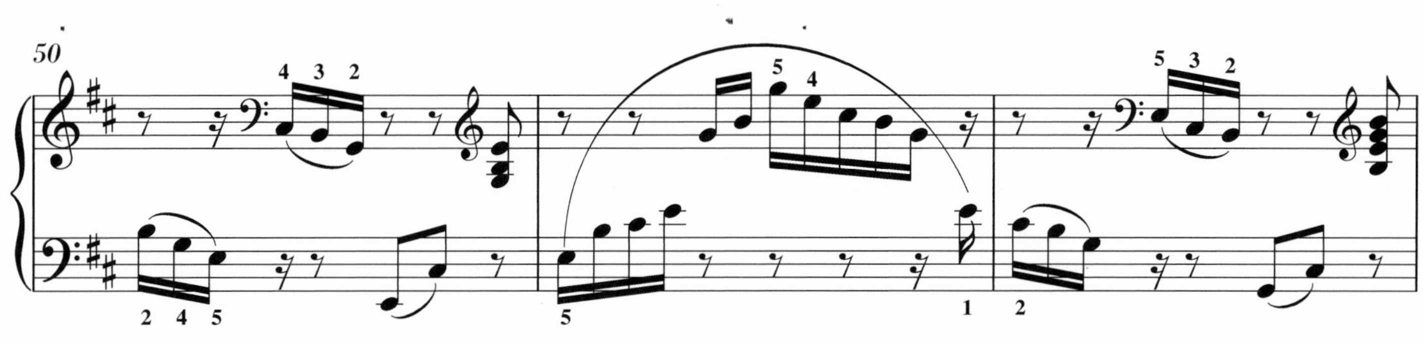
50

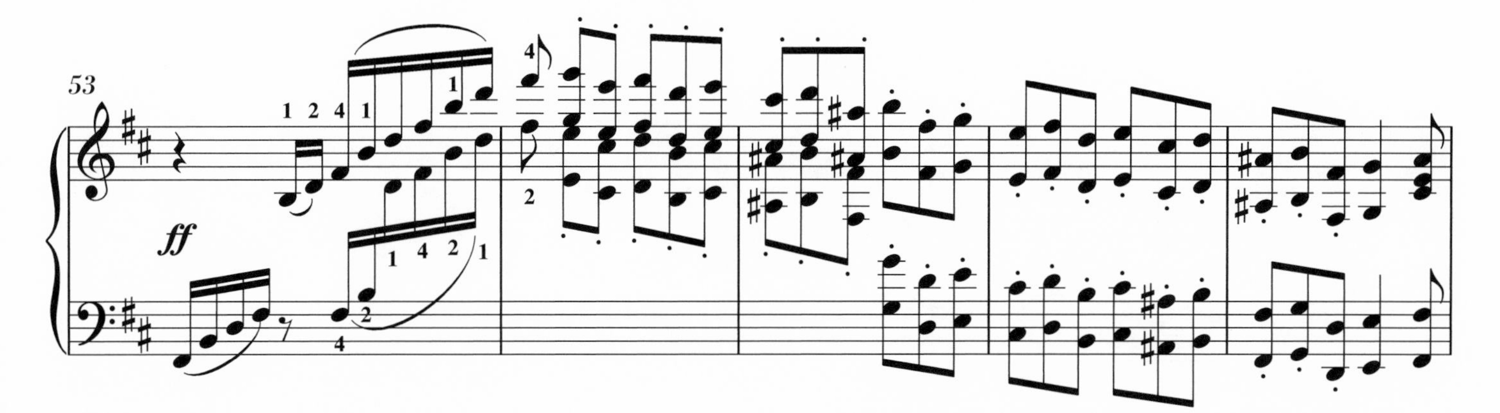
53
ff

58
mf
cresc.

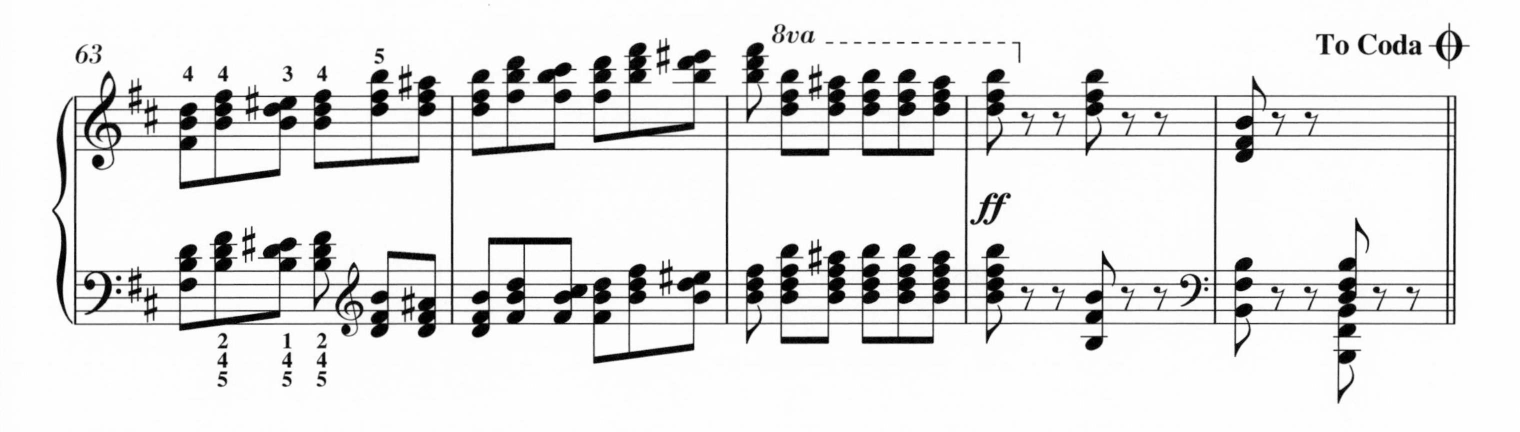
63
8va
To Coda
ff

Dolce cantabile

* The LH can be played by the RH if the interval is too big. Don't arpeggiate.

99
p (a tempo)

106
poco cresc.
mf

113
p

120
pp

126
D.S. al Coda
Tempo I
p

CODA

September: The Hunt
Сентябрь: Охота
Sentiabr': Okhota

Пора, пора! Рога трубят;
Псари в охотничьих уборах
Чем свет уж на конях сидят;
Борзые прыгают на сворах.
А. Пушкин

It is time! The horns are sounding!
The hunters in their hunting dress
are mounted on their horses;
in early dawn the borzois are jumping.
Aleksandr Pushkin

Pyotr Il'yich Tchaikovsky
Op. 37bis, No. 9

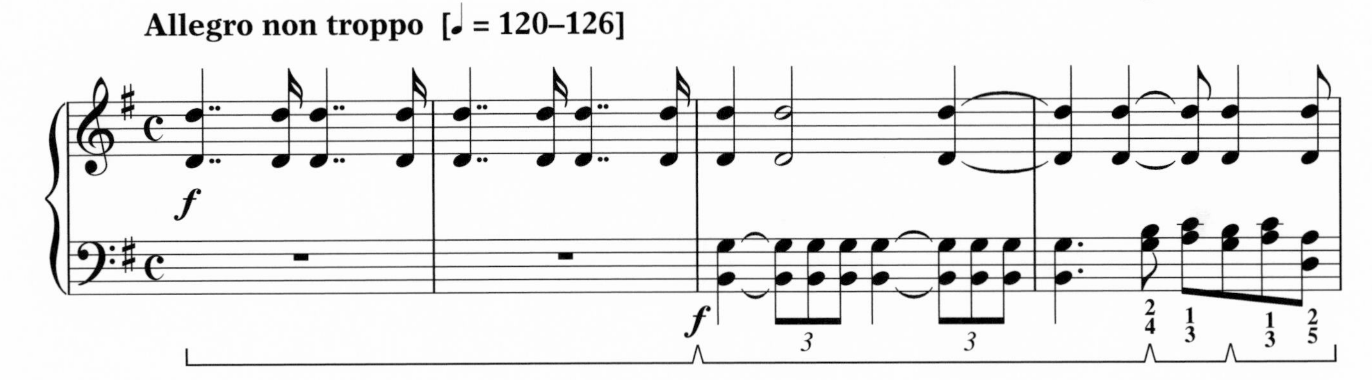

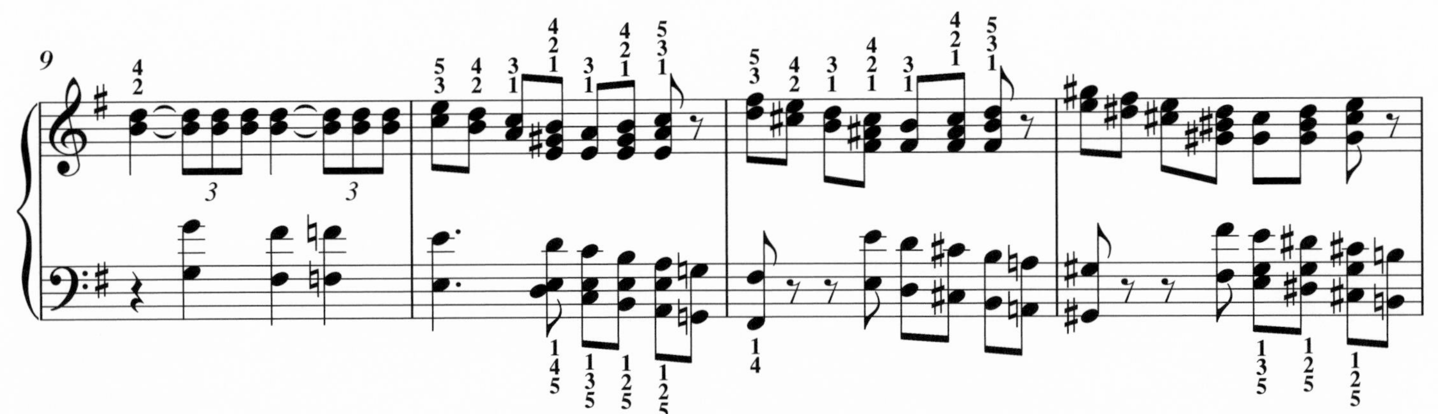

17
ff

20

23

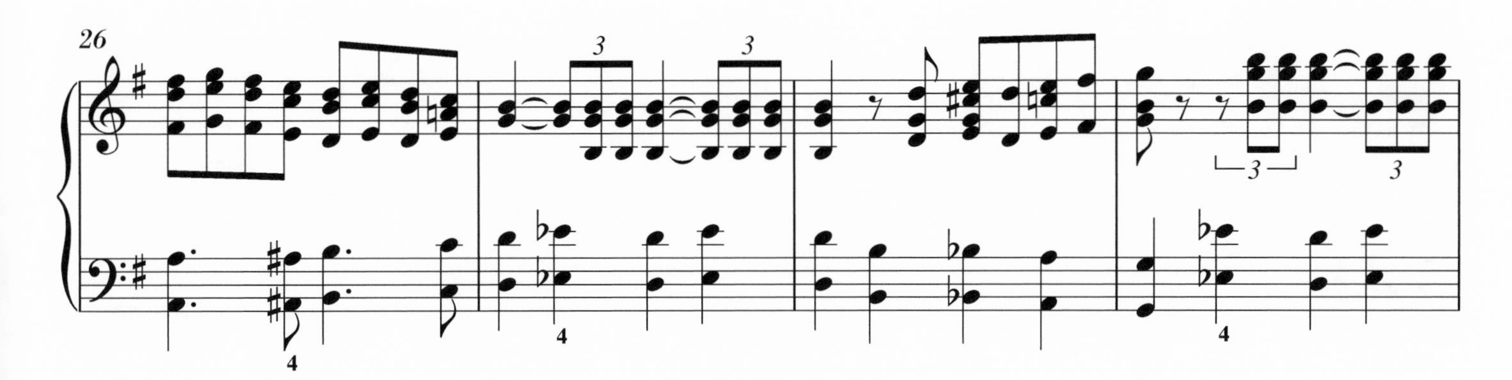
26

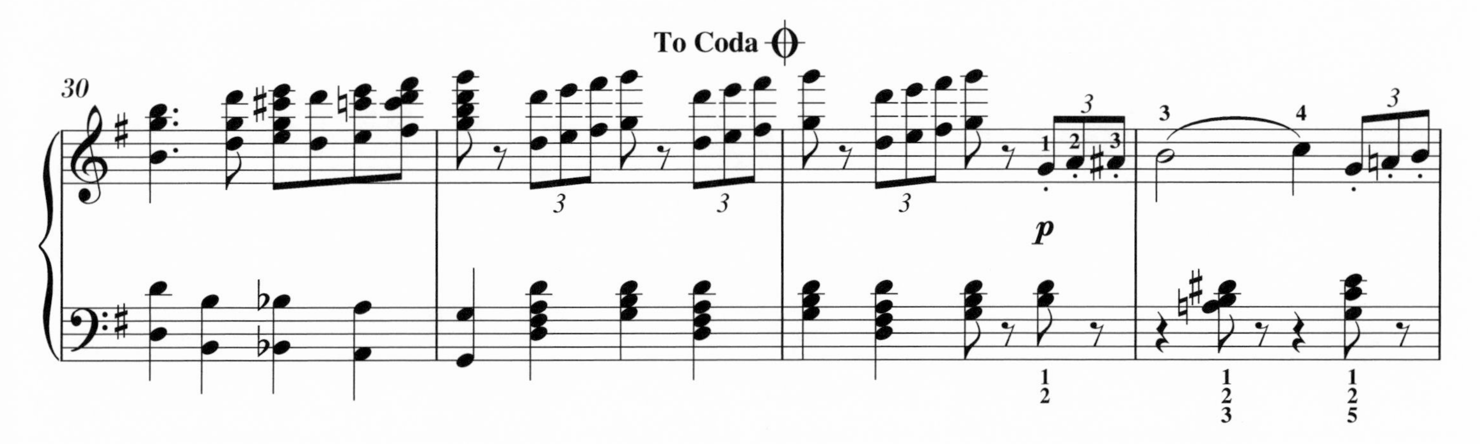
To Coda
30
p

34
(LH above)

38
poco cresc.

42
mf
p

45

48
poco a poco crescendo

51

54
f

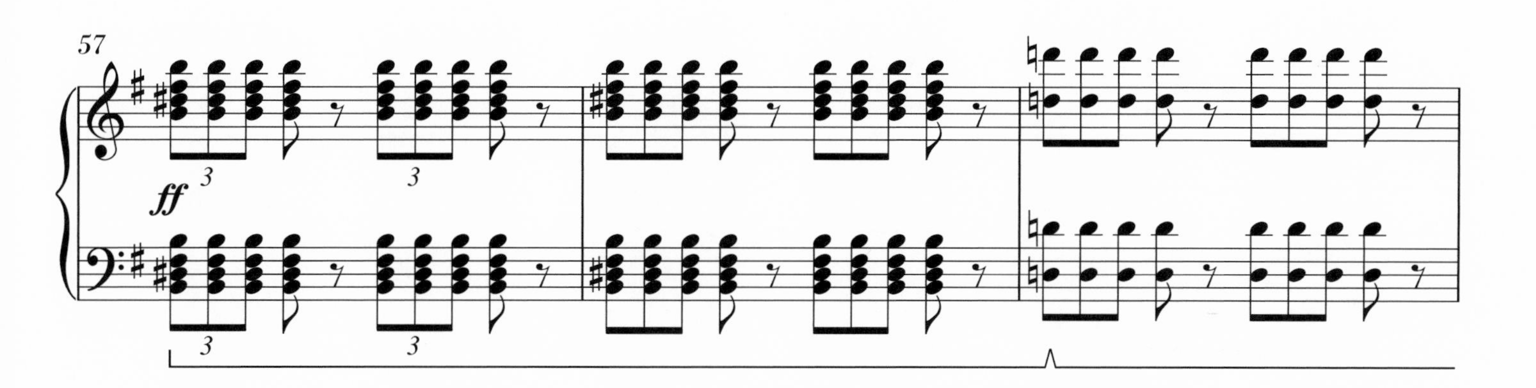
57
ff

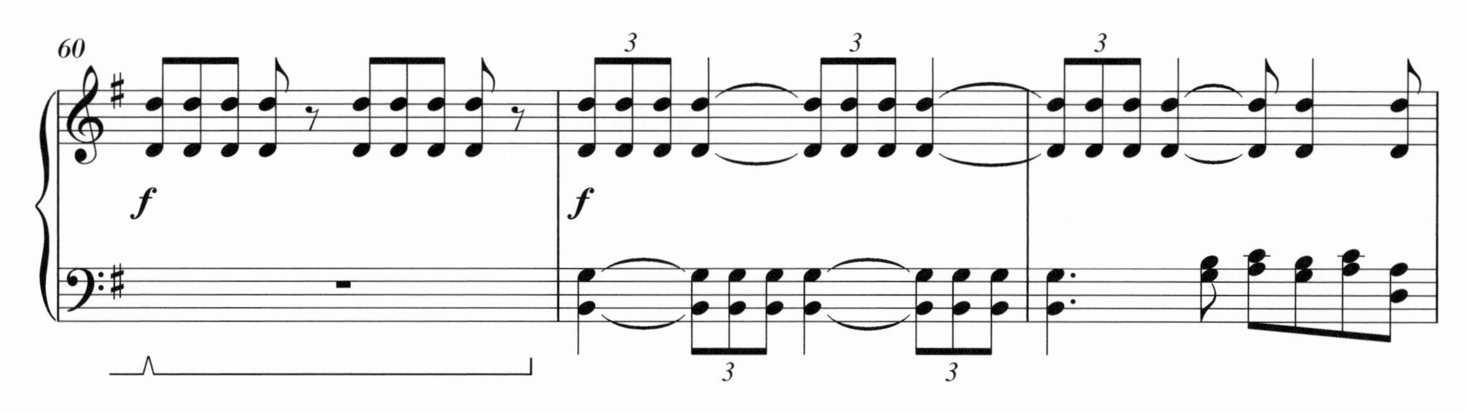
60
f
f

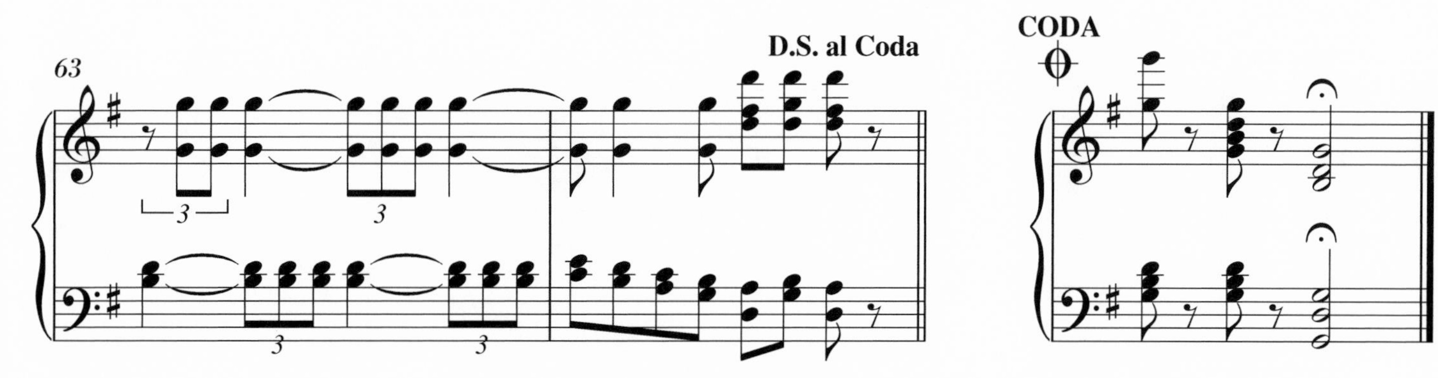
63
D.S. al Coda

CODA

October: Autumn Song
Октябрь: Осенняя песнь
Oktiabr': Osenniaia pesn'

Осень! Осыпается весь наш бедный сад,
Листья пожелтевшие по ветру летят...
А. Толстой

Autumn, falling down on our poor orchard,
The yellow leaves are flying in the wind.
Aleksey Nikolayevich Tolstoy

Pyotr Il'yich Tchaikovsky
Op. 37bis, No. 10

dim.
r.h.
l.h.

(poco più mosso)
p

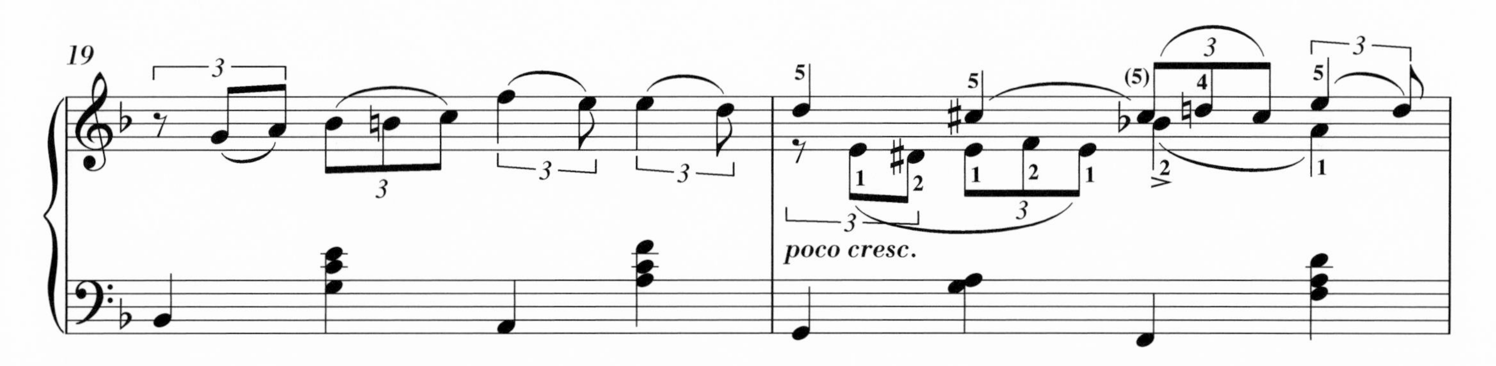
poco cresc.

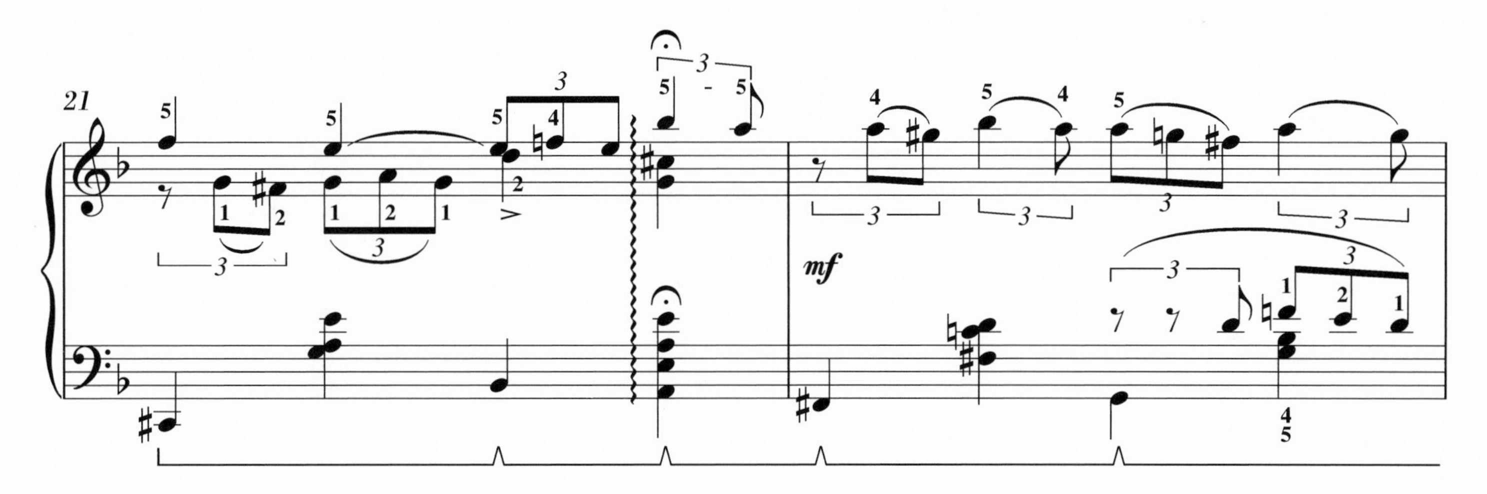
mf

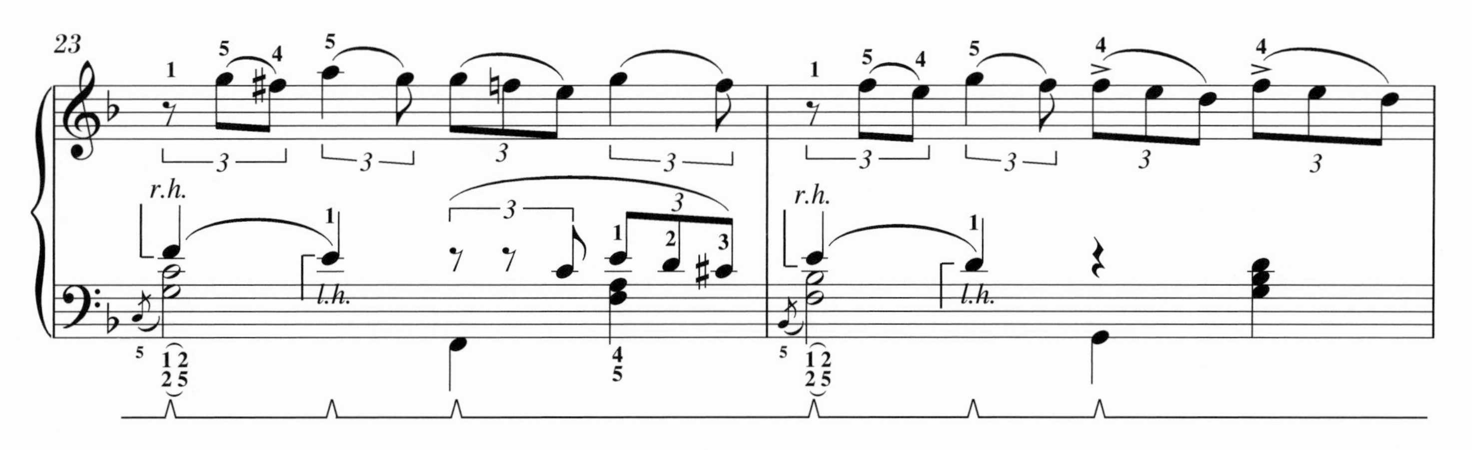
r.h.
l.h.
r.h.
l.h.

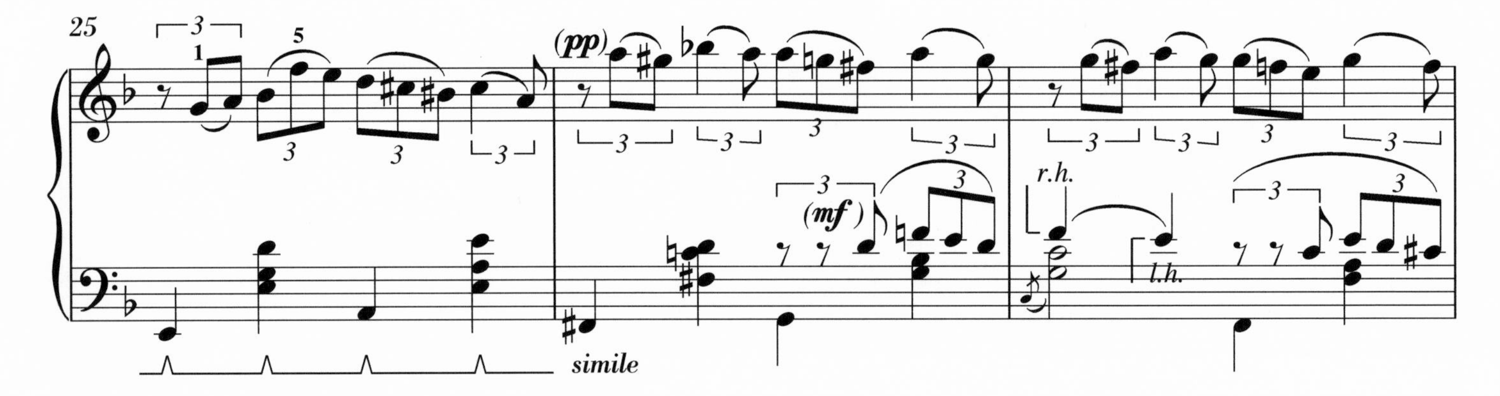
25
(pp)
(mf)
r.h.
l.h.
simile

28
r.h.
l.h.
p

31
riten.

34
a tempo
p

38
poco cresc.

41
dim.
p marcato

44
r.h.
poco più f

47

50
pp

53
morendo
pppp

November: Troika
Ноябрь: На тройке
Noiabr': Na troike

Не гляди же с тоской на дорогу,
И за тройкой во след не спеши,
И тоскливую в сердце тревогу
Поскорей навсегда заглуши.
Н. Некрасов

In your loneliness do not look at the road,
and do not rush out after the troika.
Suppress at once and forever
the fear of longing in your heart.
Nikolai Nekrasov

Pyotr Il'yich Tchaikovsky
Op. 37bis, No. 11

Allegro moderato [♩ = 110–120]

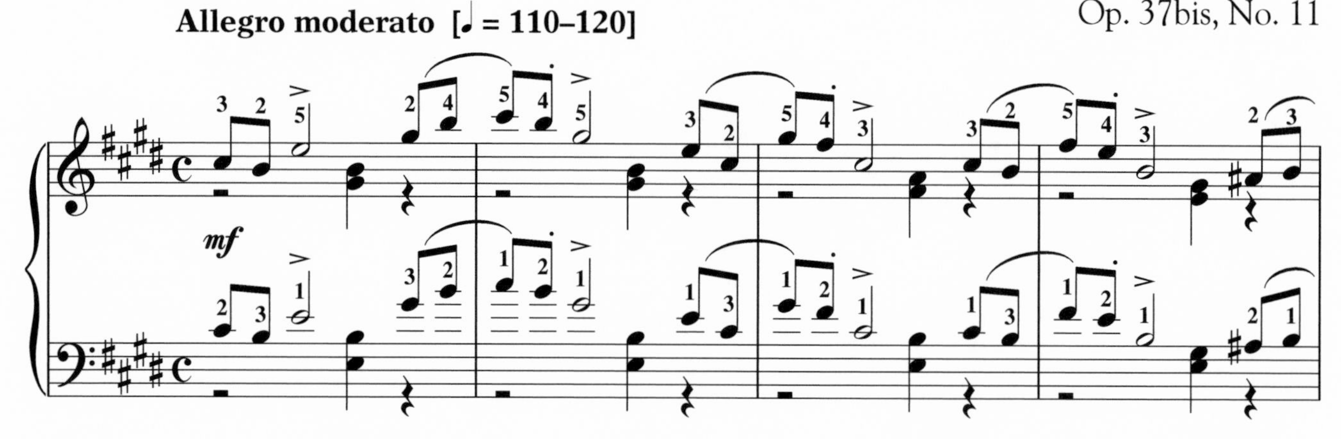

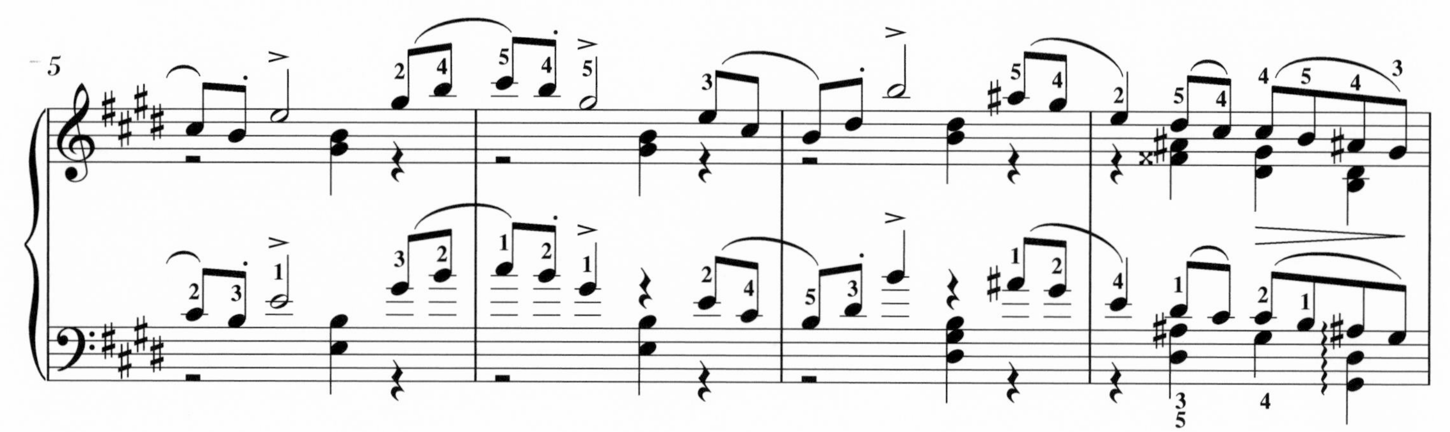

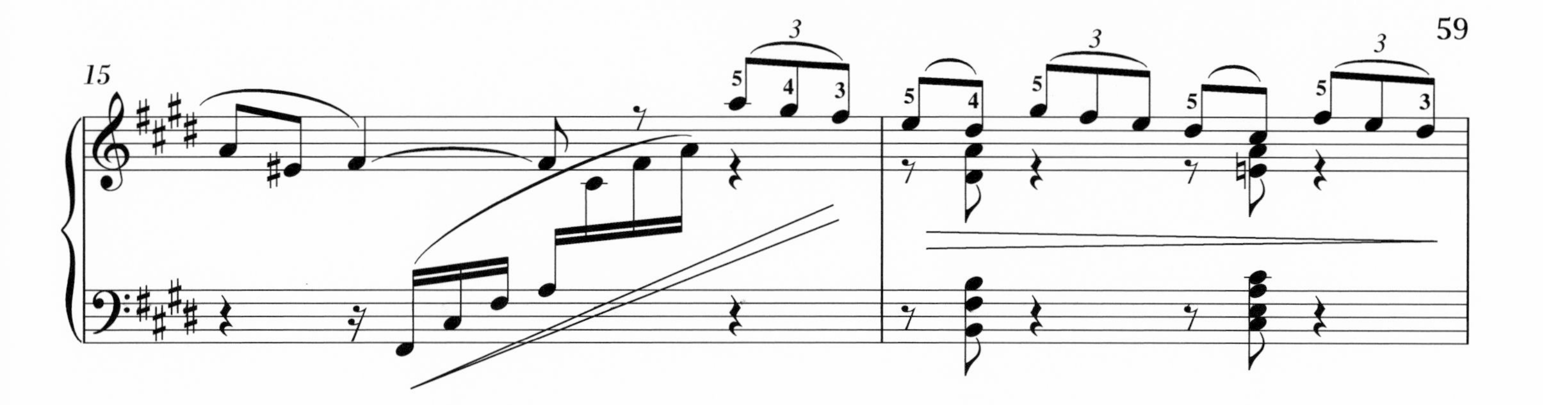

cresc.

dim.

* This is the only fingering indication by Tchaikovsky in the entire cycle.

41
p
sf
mf
sf

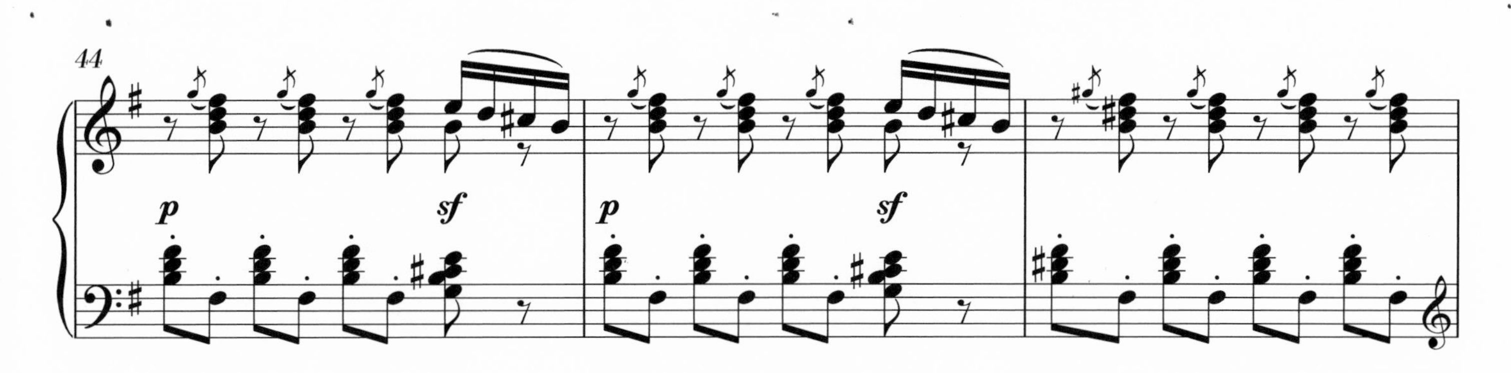
44
p
sf
p
sf

47

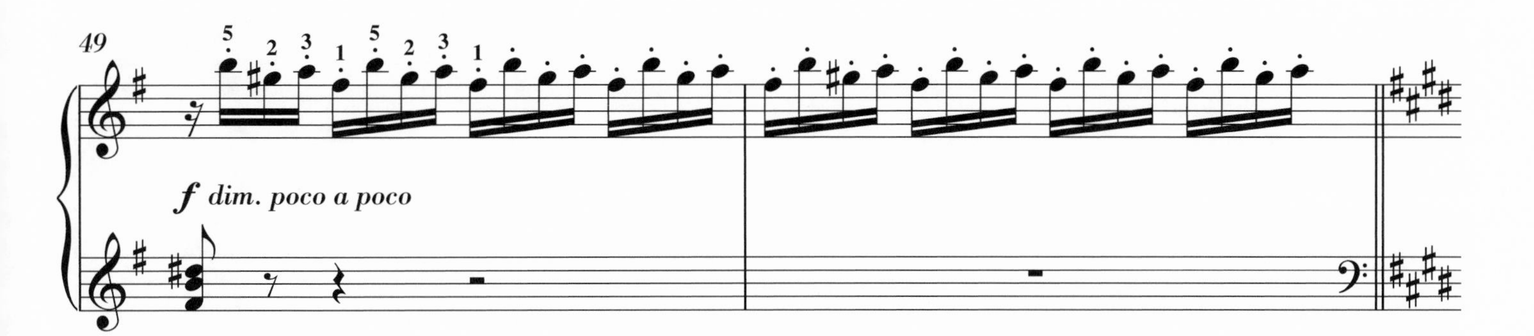
49
f dim. poco a poco

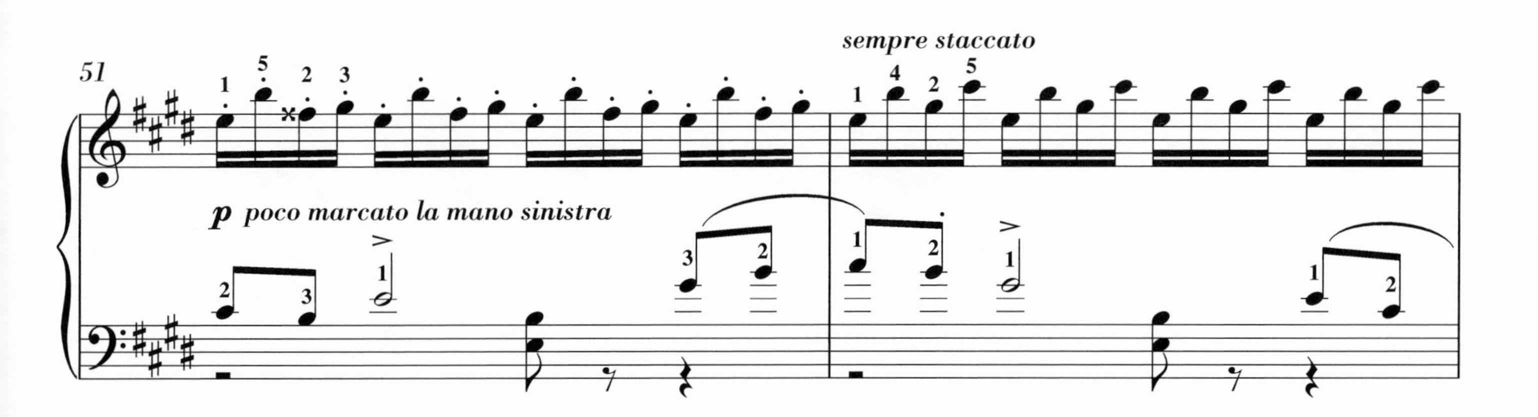
51
sempre staccato
p poco marcato la mano sinistra

53

55

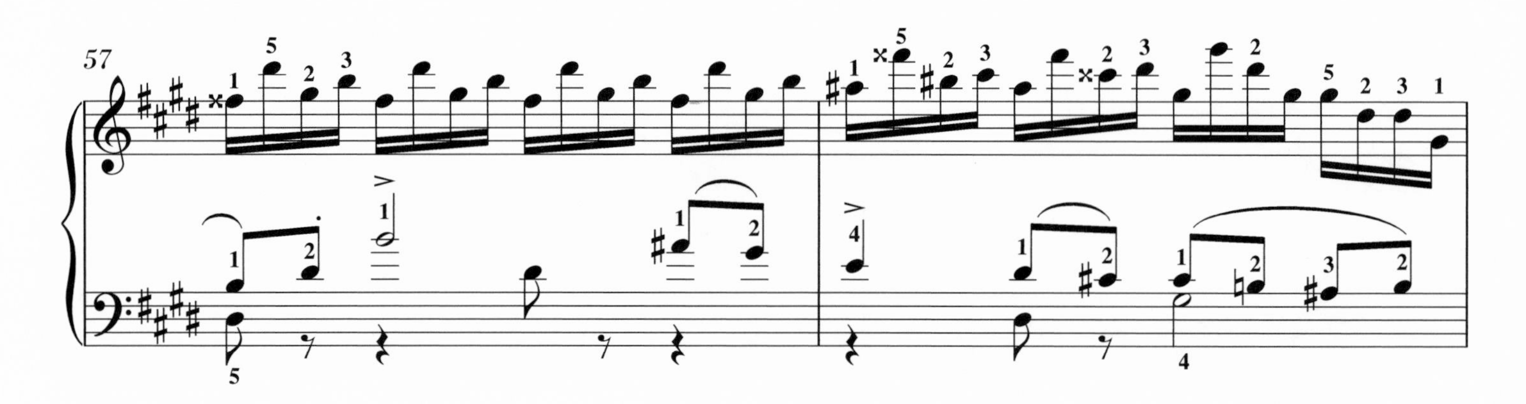
57

59
p espr.

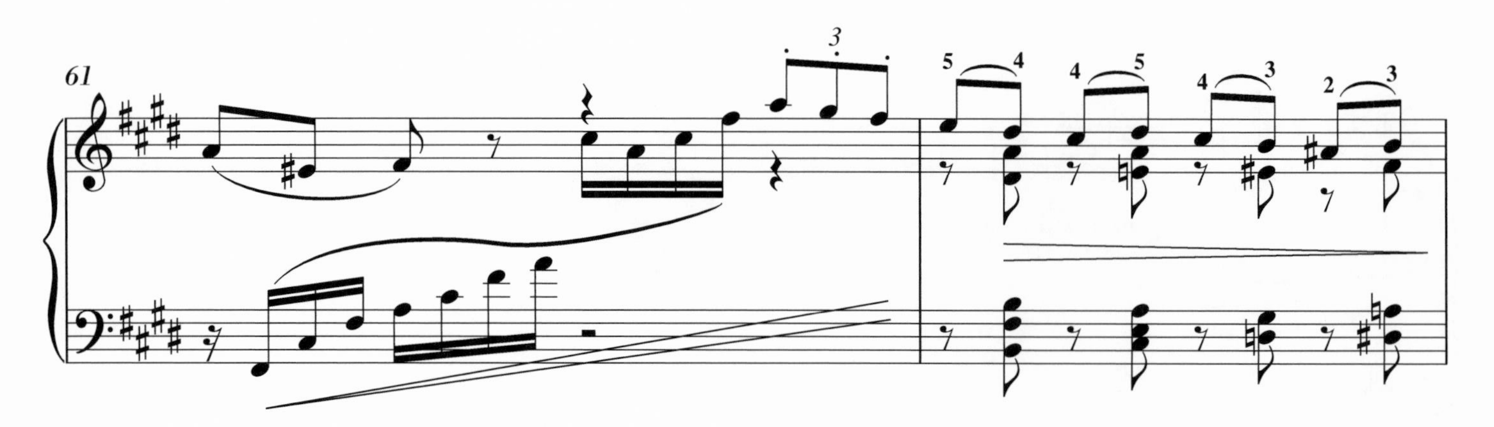
61

63

65

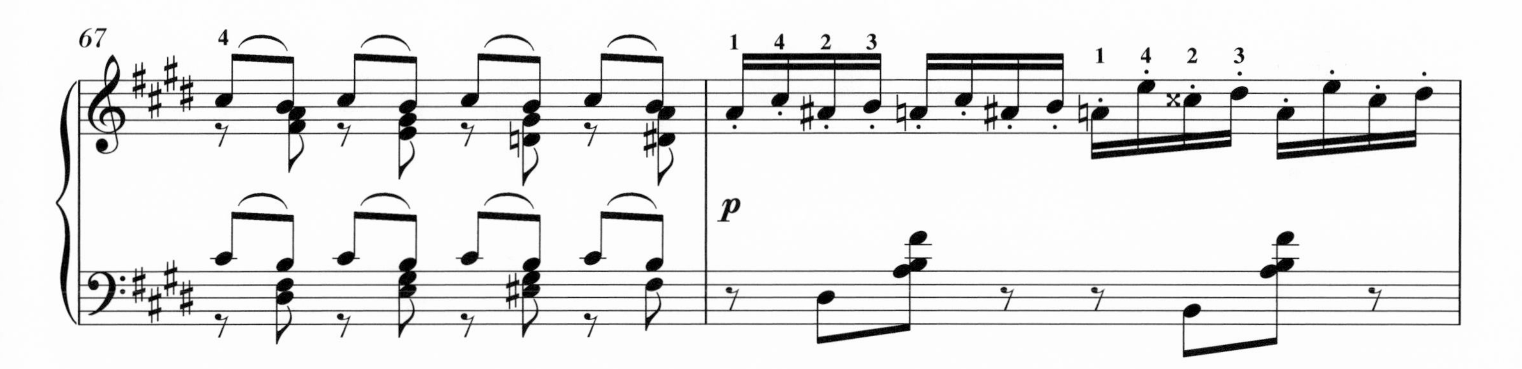
67
p

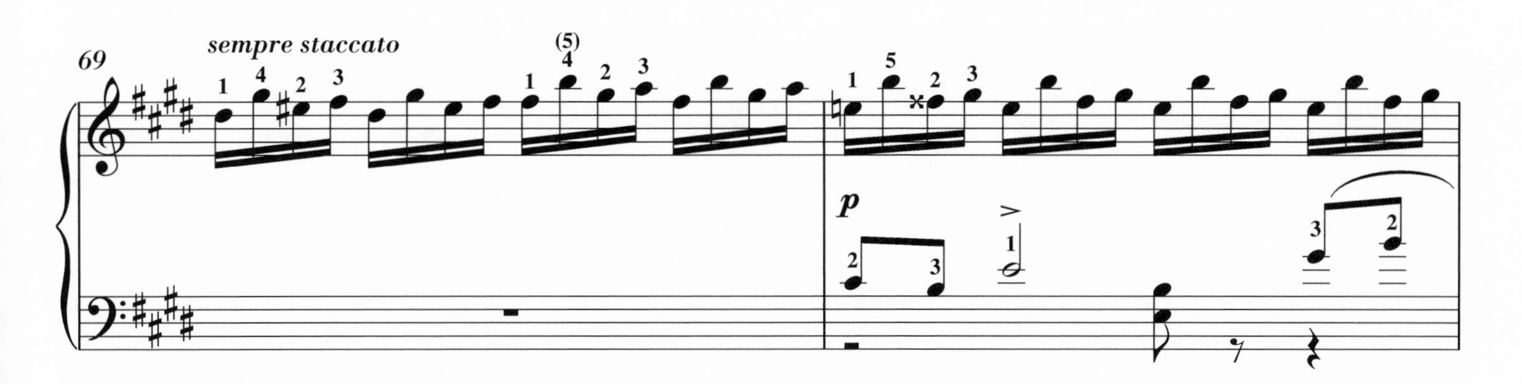
69
sempre staccato
p

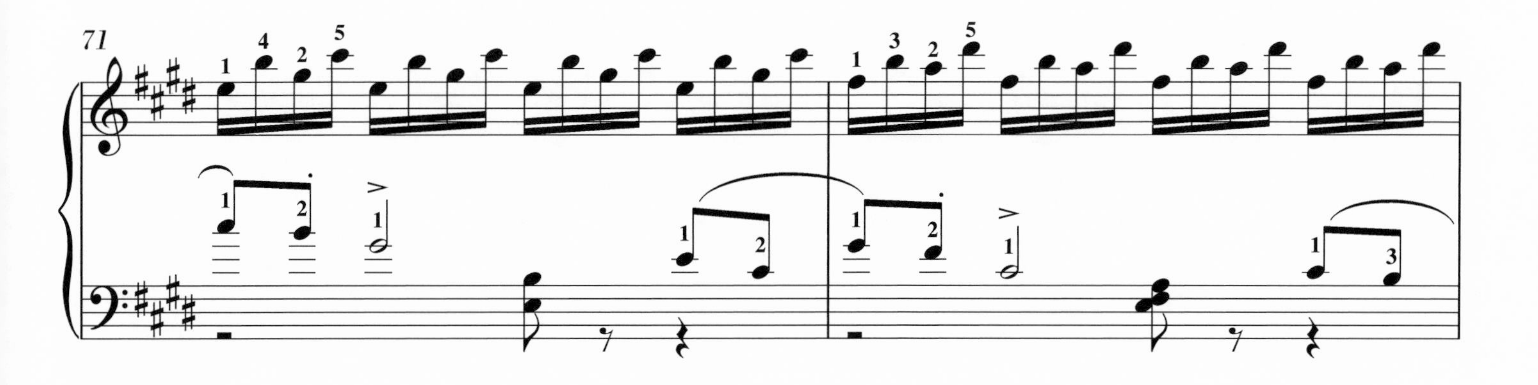
71

73

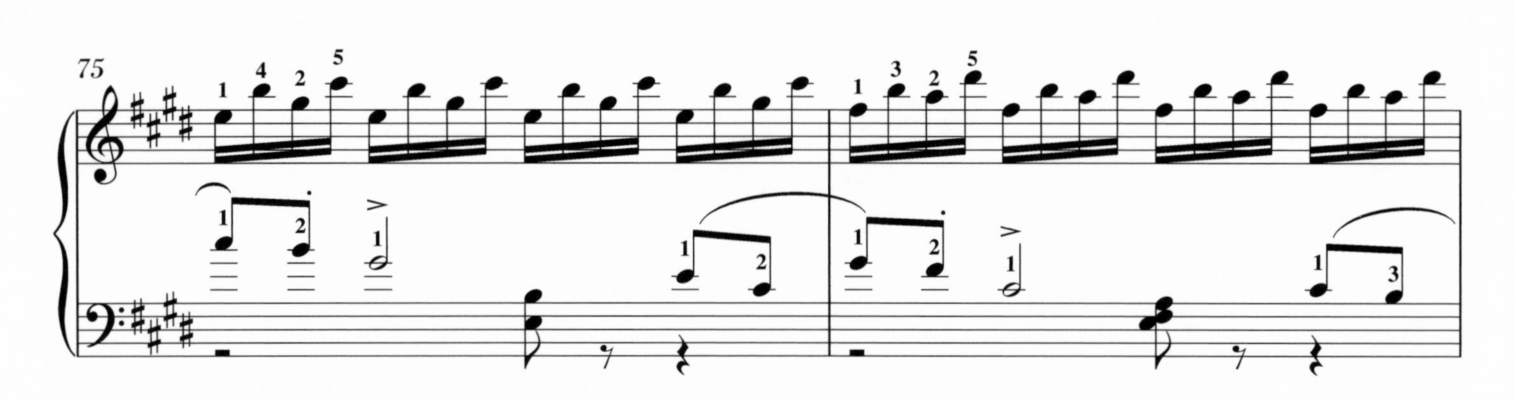
75

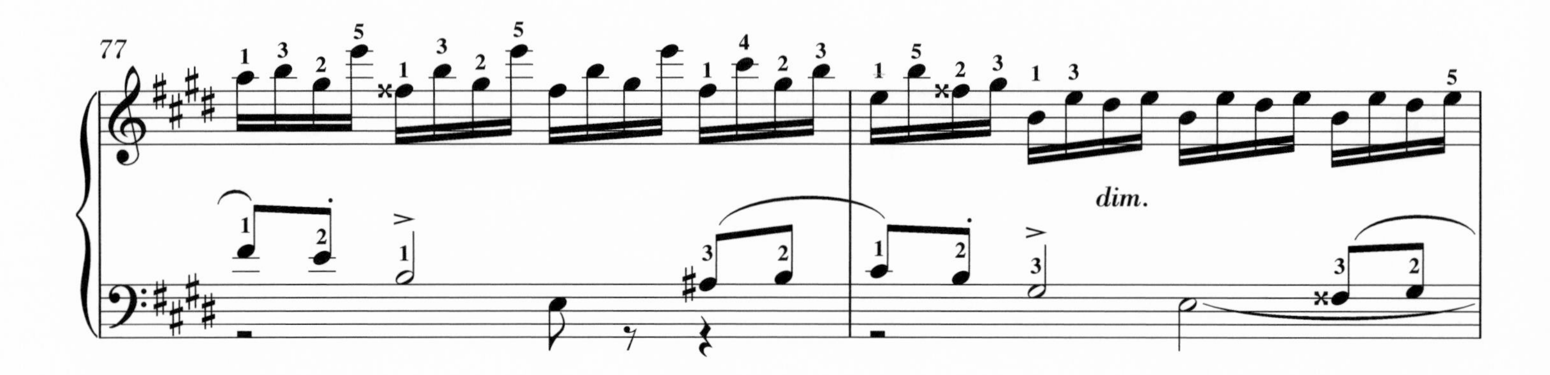
77
dim.

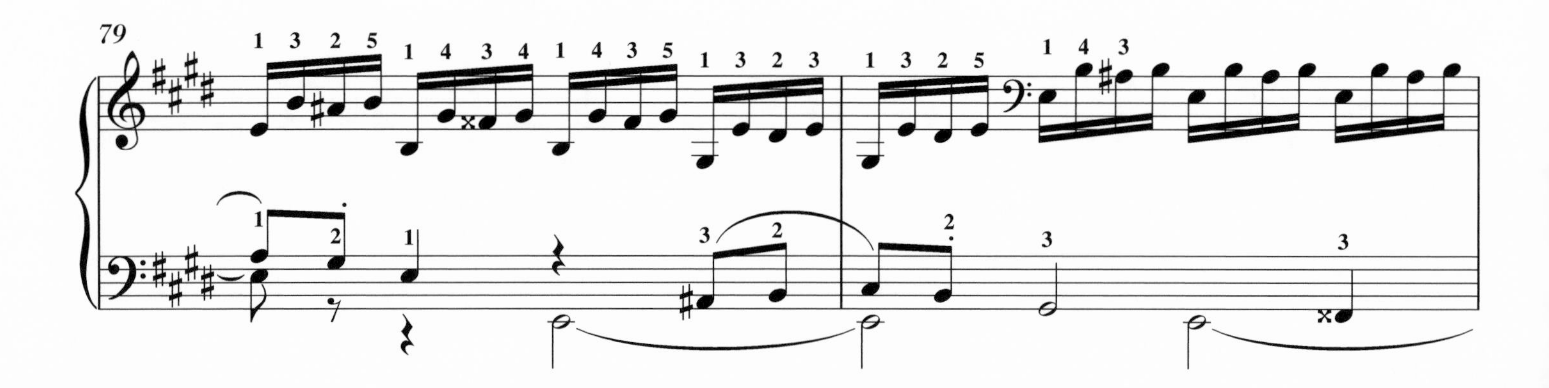
79

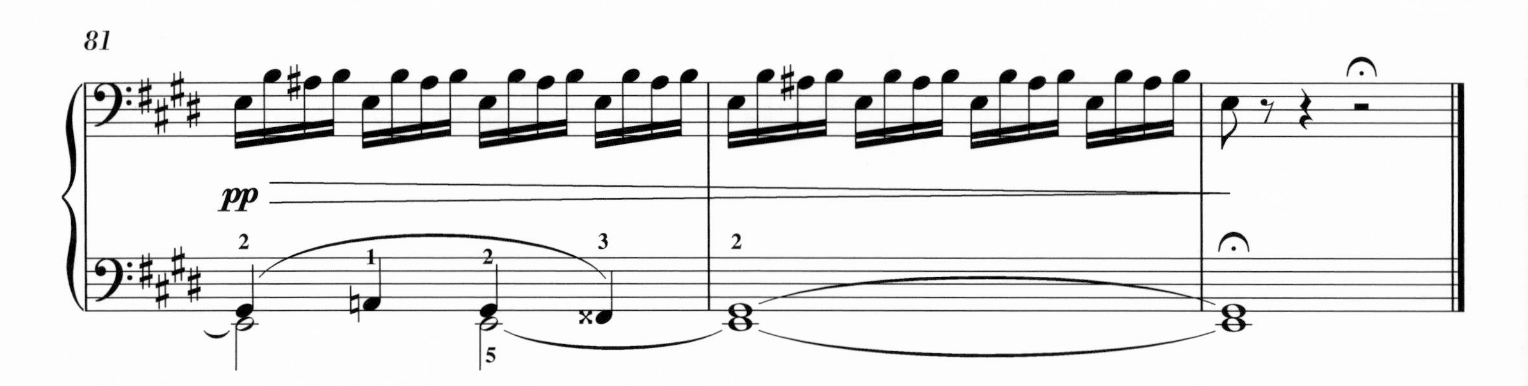
81
pp

December: Christmas
Декабрь: Святки
Dekabr': Sviatky

Раз в крещенский вечерок
Девушки гадали:
За ворота башмачок,
Сняв с ноги, бросали.
В. Жуковский

Once upon a Christmas night
the girls were telling fortunes:
taking their slippers off their feet
and throwing them out of the gate.
Vasily Zhukovsky

Pyotr Il'yich Tchaikovsky
Op. 37bis, No. 12

Tempo di Valse [𝅗𝅥. = 62–68]

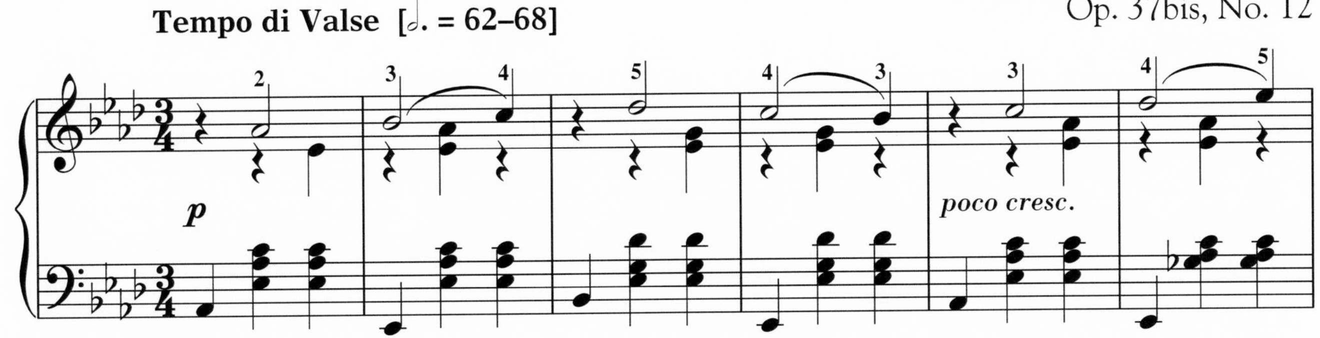

24
a tempo
p

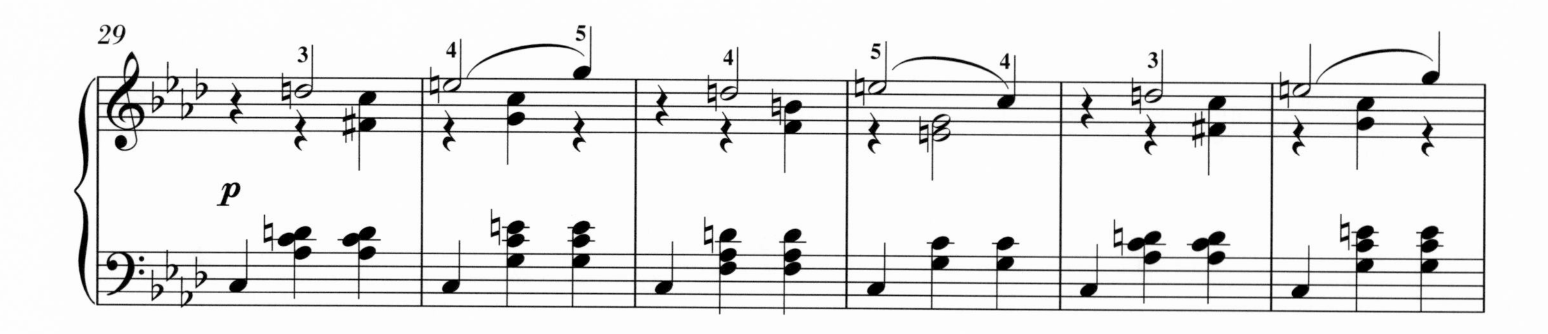
29
p

35
p

40
p
mf

45
p

50
mf
dim.

55
p

61
molto riten.
a tempo
p

66

72

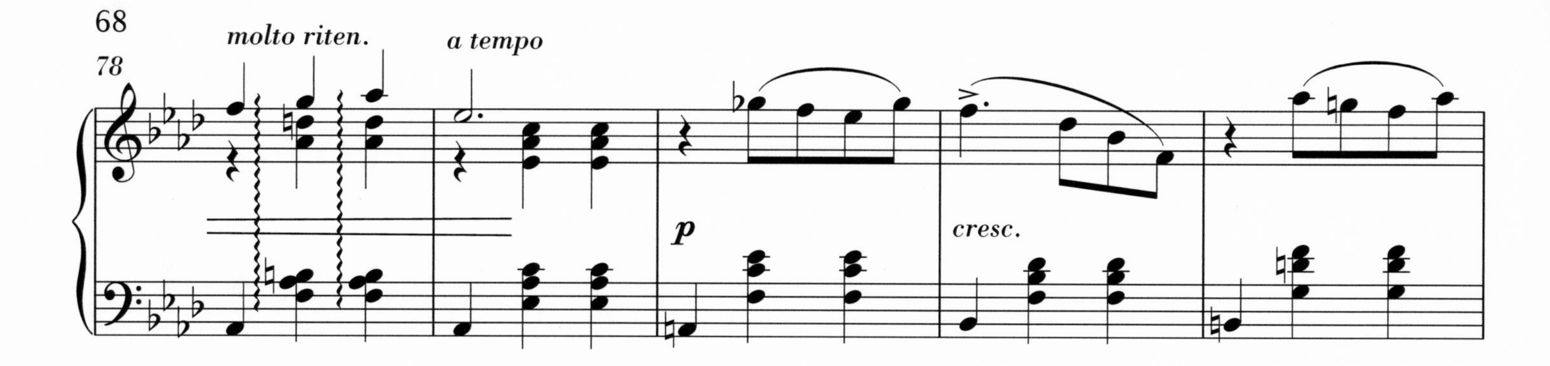
78
molto riten.
a tempo
p
cresc.

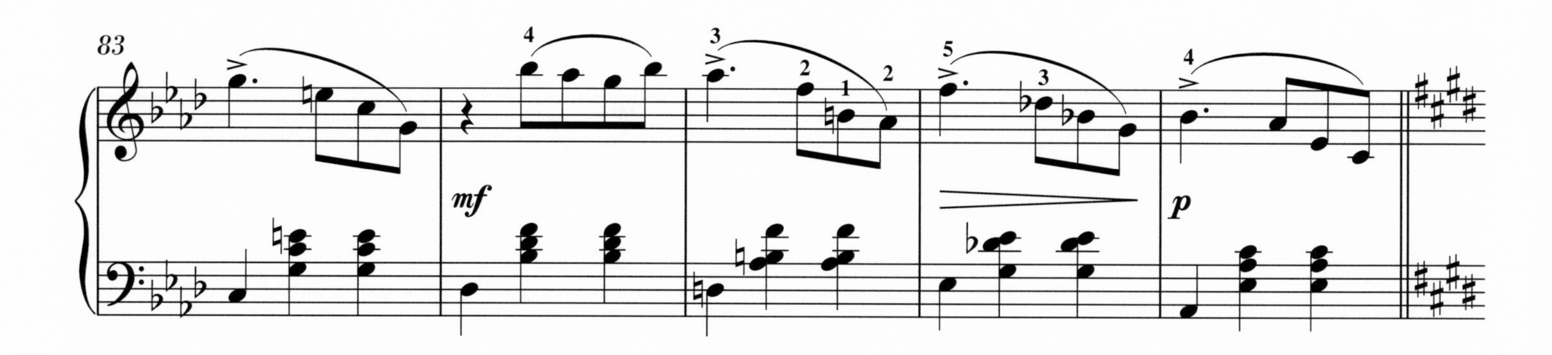
83
mf
p

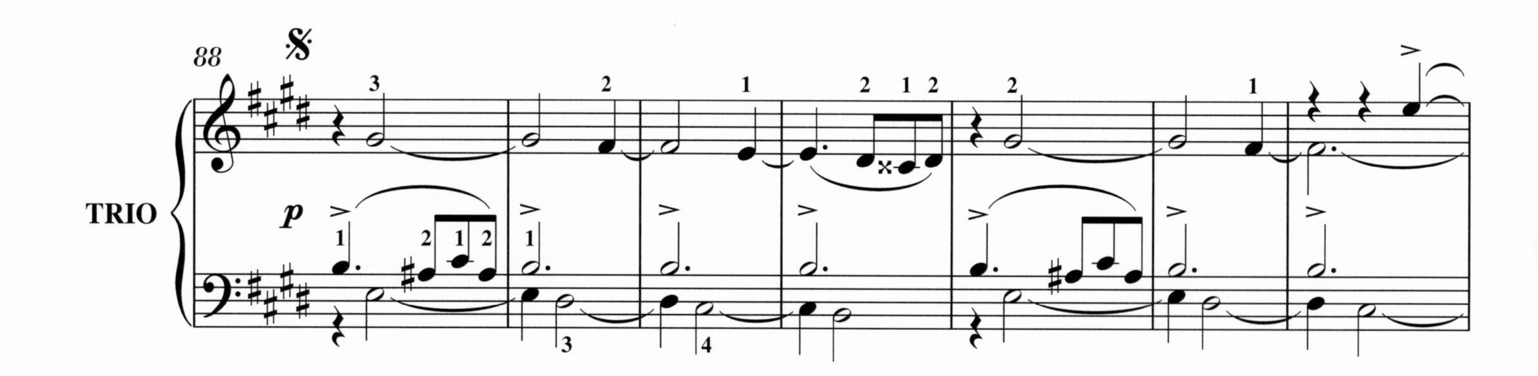
88
TRIO
p

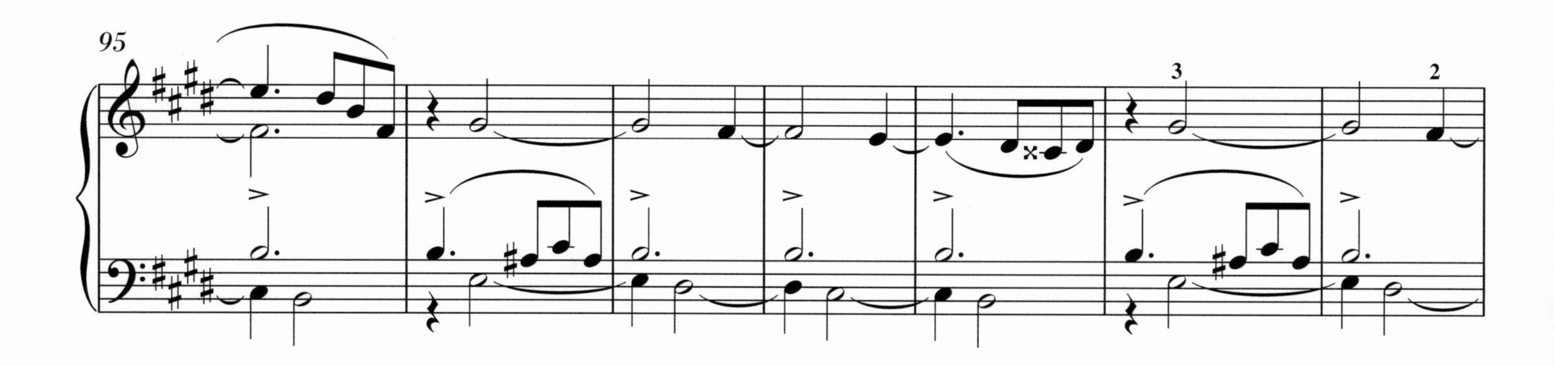
95

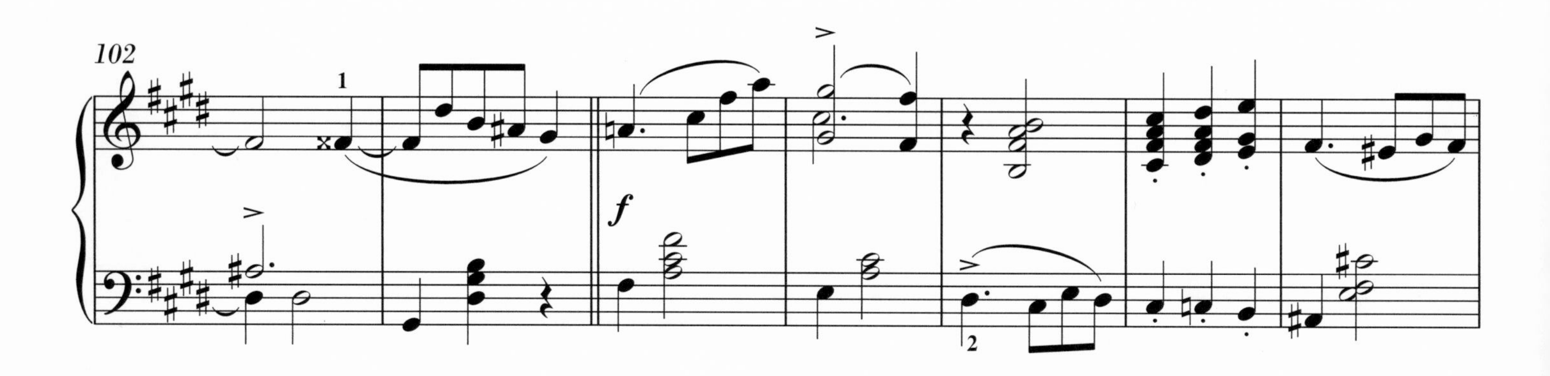
102
f

109

116
p

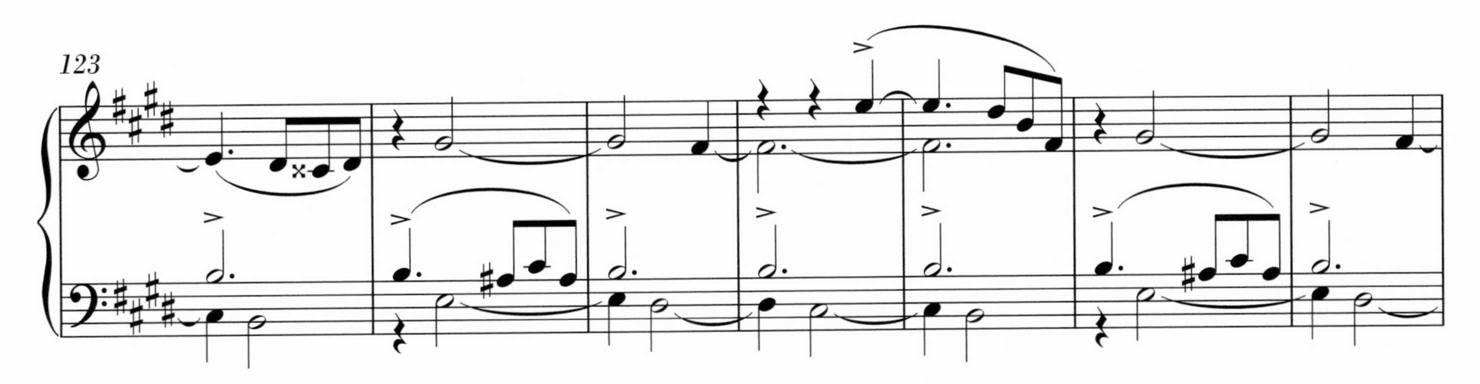
123

130
poco cresc.

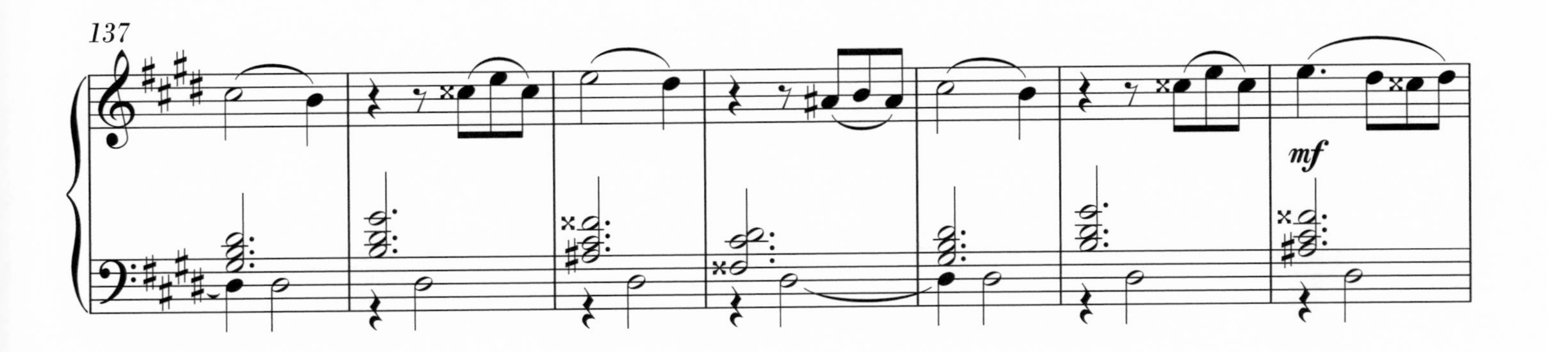
137
mf

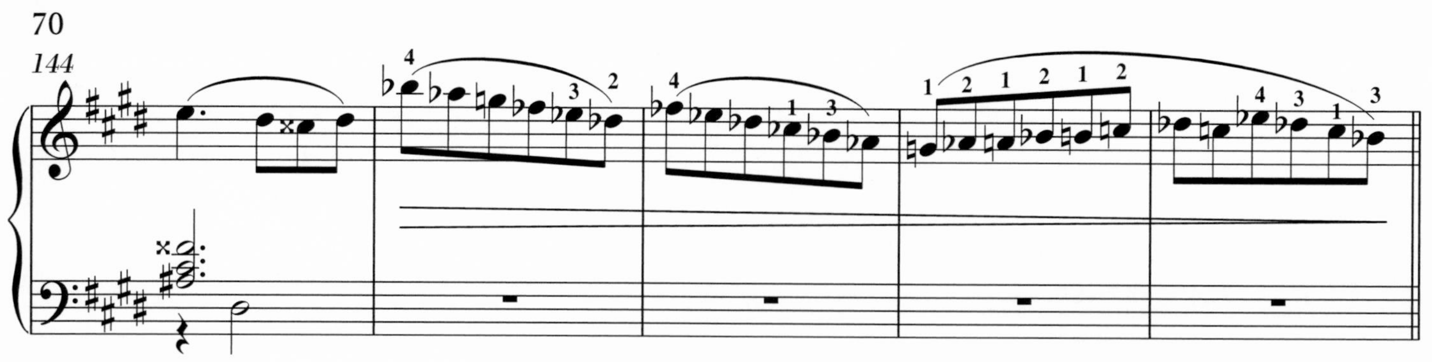
144
Da Capo al segno e poi Coda

149
CODA
p
poco a poco cresc.

157

165
f
mf

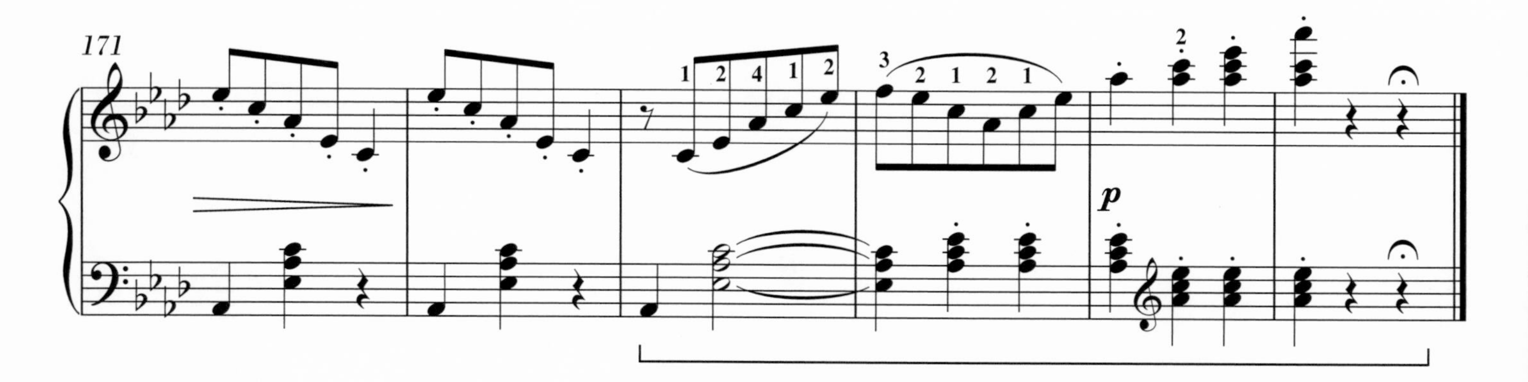
171
p

ABOUT THE EDITOR

Alexandre Dossin

Considered by Martha Argerich an "extraordinary musician" and by international critics a "phenomenon" and "a master of contrasts," Alexandre Dossin keeps active performing, recording, and teaching careers.

Born in Brazil, where he lived until he was nineteen, Dossin spent nine years studying in Moscow, Russia, before establishing residency in the United States. This background allows him to be fluent in several languages and equally comfortable in a wide range of piano repertoire.

Currently on the faculty of the University of Oregon School of Music, Dossin is a graduate from the University of Texas-Austin and the Moscow Tchaikovsky Conservatory in Russia. He studied with and was an assistant of Sergei Dorensky at the Tchaikovsky Conservatory, and William Race and Gregory Allen at UT-Austin.

A prizewinner in several international piano competitions, Dossin received the First Prize and the Special Prize at the 2003 Martha Argerich International Piano Competition in Buenos Aires, Argentina. Other awards include the Silver Medal and Second Honorable Mention in the Maria Callas Grand Prix and Third Prize and Special Prize in the Mozart International Piano Competition.

He performed numerous live recitals for public radio in Texas, Wisconsin, and Illinois, including returning engagements at the Dame Myra Hess Memorial Concert Series. Dossin has performed in over twenty countries, including international festivals in Japan, Canada, the United States, Brazil, and Argentina, on some occasions sharing the stage with Martha Argerich. He was a soloist with the Brazilian Symphony, Buenos Aires Philharmonic, Mozarteum Symphony, and São Paulo Symphony, having collaborated with renowned conductors such as Charles Dutoit, Michael Gielen, Isaac Karabtchevsky, Keith Clark, and Eleazar de Carvalho.

Dossin has CDs released by Musicians Showcase Recording (2002), Blue Griffin (*A Touch of Brazil*, 2005), and Naxos (*Verdi-Liszt Paraphrases*, 2007; *Kabalevsky Complete Sonatas and Sonatinas*, 2009; *Kabalevsky Complete Preludes*, 2009; *Russian Transcriptions*, 2012), praised in reviews by *Diapason*, *The Financial Times*, *Fanfare Magazine*, *American Record Guide*, *Clavier* and other international publications.

In the United States, Alexandre Dossin was featured as the main interview and on the cover of *Clavier* magazine and interviewed by *International Piano Magazine* (South Korea). He is an editor and recording artist for several Schirmer Performance Editions.

Dossin is a member of the Board of Directors for the American Liszt Society and the President of the Oregon Chapter of the American Liszt Society. He lives in the beautiful south hills of Eugene with his wife Maria, and children Sophia and Victor.

www.dossin.net